FUTURE PROOF YOUR MARKETING

FUTURE PROOF YOUR MARKETING

HOW TO GROW YOUR BUSINESS WITH

DIGITAL MARKETING NOW AND DURING

THE ARTIFICIAL INTELLIGENCE REVOLUTION

KEVIN GETCH

LIONCREST
PUBLISHING

FUTURE PROOF YOUR MARKETING

How to Grow Your Business with Digital Marketing Now
and During the Artificial Intelligence Revolution

ISBN   978-1-5445-0416-2 *Hardcover*

978-1-5445-0415-5 *Paperback*

978-1-5445-0414-8 *Ebook*

*Creating this book for you, the reader, is a culmination of my
life's learnings, struggles, mistakes, successes, and so many
amazing moments. I couldn't have done this without the drive to
help other people that my mother instilled in me. She taught me
about the ripple effect and how dropping a single pebble into a
pond can create thousands and thousands of ripples across the
entire pond, and how our actions every day, whether positive
or negative, are impacting the world. It is part of my purpose in
this life to continue the amazing positive ripple that she started
and help turn it into a wave of positive action in this world.*

*To my amazing wife, who is an all-around badass, a
beautiful warrior, business owner, mother, and best friend
whom I look up to and lean on. I'm eternally grateful to have
found you, Jennifer. You love me unconditionally and you
make me a better person. I'm so happy to be living the life
of my dreams alongside you, the woman of my dreams!*

*To my children, Mariah and Brandon. Inspiration comes from
the most unique places, and you have inspired me to be the
best man, father, and person I can be. You're a big part of what
drives me to help make this world a little better each day.*

*I also want to thank my work family. To the entire team at
Webfor, thank you for your passion, dedication, and for being
amazing people who help make this world a better place. All of
you make Webfor the amazing organization that it is, where we
get to do what we love and do it with the people we love being
around. Our purpose is to help people and make a positive impact,
and you make this possible every day by the great work you do
for our clients. This couldn't have been done without you!*

*Finally, I would like to thank all of our amazing
clients. Your trust, friendship, and partnership over the
years has helped make this possible. I look forward to
continuing to serve you for many more years to come.*

CONTENTS

INTRODUCTION 9

PART I: THE CURRENT MARKETING LANDSCAPE

1. YOU ARE HERE 23
2. WHO'S WITH YOU? 35
3. WHAT PEOPLE ARE DOING 49
4. HOW TO CREATE A CUSTOMER-CENTRIC

   STRATEGY 75

PART II: NAVIGATING A NEW MARKETING LANDSCAPE

5. WHERE THEY'RE GOING NEXT 109
6. THE THREE Ps 121
7. THE NEW DIGITAL ASSISTANT 139

CONCLUSION 153
SUPPLEMENT 159
APPENDIX...165
ABOUT THE AUTHOR 171

INTRODUCTION

ARE YOU READY?

Marketing is about to undergo a huge shift. The changes have already begun.

It wasn't that long ago that we needed to type a specific query into a search engine and scroll through pages of results to find the answer we were looking for. Now we're not at all surprised when our phone offers us a list of nearby restaurants. Soon, our digital assistants will suggest dinner at a spot that serves our favorite foods, make the reservation for us, remind us when the dinner hour approaches, and order up a self-driving car to take us there. After the meal, the assistant may pipe up and ask, "Hey, what did you think of that?"

The first time that happens, we will be amazed by what our

digital assistants can do for us. I experienced this myself recently, when faced with the daunting task of finding a picture of my elliptical machine in my files. Instead of flailing about on my computer, I used voice search. I just said the word "elliptical" out loud and my digital assistant returned the correct image. It didn't matter that the file was not named "elliptical" or that the photograph showed only part of the machine buried among other stuff in my garage. My assistant "knew" what I wanted. Amazing.

Very quickly, everyone will come to expect this type of experience, your customers included. I'm sure you already acknowledge the importance of customer experience, but you may not recognize how crucial it's about to become. **I believe customer experience will become one of the largest business-ranking factors in the next five to ten years.** Customer experience is already critical to the success of a business, but in the very near future, customer experience will *make or break* your business. If you don't comprehend that now, the new technology will not work in your favor. If you do, you open up a world of opportunity.

So, are you ready?

If your company is like most companies today, probably not.

You've probably made a good start, like one marketing

executive we worked with recently. His company recognized the importance of customer experience in the face of rapidly changing technology. They hired people to handle it, and those talented folks created great content and made a plan to publish it. That was fantastic—probably 90 percent of the people we talk to aren't even creating quality content—but they had little strategy beyond that. The executive was highly knowledgeable about marketing and automation but didn't have the internal expertise to make sure that content was optimized for maximum exposure in search engines and for tracking the success of campaigns.

They had a talented team and excellent content, but it wasn't achieving the desired results. They thought that just increasing traffic was the answer. I told them that getting tons of traffic wasn't that hard, but it might not be very good quality traffic. What the company needed wasn't just more traffic but true customer engagement. Not people searching for irrelevant keywords and arbitrarily landing on their website, but the right people, who were likely to take the action the company needed to convert them to customers.

As part of the new strategy we helped them develop, they put in place a better plan to track effectiveness, improved the customer experience, optimized their content to be found in search engines, optimized their paid ad campaigns, and reclaimed over 3,000 high-value links that weren't properly redirected to their website. Without creating any additional content, their website visits grew by 37 percent, and conversions rose 33 percent over the same month in the prior year. Even better, their company started experiencing enormous growth.

This was a very successful, driven international company, moving forward all the time and swimming fast. They were working hard and doing many things right, but some of their technique was off. Heck, it hadn't occurred to them that maybe they could stop swimming so hard and build a boat. This strategy would make sure they kept on moving efficiently and get where they wanted to go.

The truth is, many companies aren't even swimming. At best, they are treading water. They are not only unaware of how digital marketing is about to change, but they also probably don't have a good handle on their current marketing strategy. If they don't catch up as technology and consumer behavior evolves, they're going to be left behind.

Whether you're off to a strong start and wonder how you can improve your performance, or you feel like you're flailing around in uncharted waters, keep reading. No matter your starting point, you'll learn how to optimize your current marketing and prepare for the sea of change to come.

SAYS WHO?

Why should you listen to me? Is it because I'm Webfor's founder and Director of Digital Strategy and have helped hundreds of businesses grow and succeed? Or because I have over sixteen years of experience in marketing and speak to audiences around the country on how to grow their businesses through digital marketing? Those things tell you something about me, but it's my passion for helping people reach their goals that I really want to share with you.

That passion was so strong that I decided to trade in my job with a six-figure income and excellent benefits at a Fortune 100 company for no income and no benefits. It was 2009 in the wake of the Great Recession, not exactly the best time economically to start a business, especially with a family and a mortgage, but I simply had to. Every day I went in to work, it ate away at me. Too many times, I'd seen the marketing agency I worked for make big promises and fail to deliver on them. I decided I would rather make half as much doing something I loved and have a positive impact than to continue working there. So I made the leap into uncharted waters.

During that first year on my own, my income was actually less than half as much. I was working eighty hours a week and making a lot of sacrifices, and so was my family. But it started to get better. After a few years, I started hiring people who were better than me at everything—content strategists, SEO specialists, conversion rate optimization specialists, social media experts, paid media specialists, and website designers. Today, we have fifteen people on our team. Having that diversity was important to me.

You probably know the old saying, "If all you have is a hammer, everything looks like a nail." We didn't want that. By having so many specialists, we were making sure that our clients received solutions that actually worked for them; we offered the right mix of capabilities so we could maximize their internal expertise, allowing them to be as effective as possible. This is why I started my own business in the first place.

At Webfor, we don't say, "You need this, this, and this— because that's our package." Maybe they *don't* need all of that. Marketing needs to be tailored and customized to the client's specific needs. We don't offer cookie-cutter solutions.

My favorite early clients were people you wouldn't expect to show up at a marketing agency's door—Kathy and Sharon, a couple of teachers. These women had started an amazing preschool, but their enrollment was slipping, even though they were putting all of their time and energy into it.

The school was excellent, and they knew it. So what was going on?

The trouble was, they had a fantastic product, but the people who needed it didn't know about it. The school had done some print media, but the world was quickly shifting to digital. They hadn't yet adapted.

I loved that little school. My son went there, so I offered to trade services with Kathy and Sharon. We started doing SEO, and within a little over a year, they had a waiting list. They hired more people, reduced their own hours, and got to spend more time with their grandchildren, which was really important to them. That's the sort of outcome I live for.

Helping Kathy and Sharon made me fall even more deeply in love with my work. It made me realize we weren't just helping a business—we were helping people. We not only helped two women with a vision but all the people they hired and their families, and the community around the school. To this day, when we bring on a client, I talk to my employees about this ripple effect and the responsibility we're taking on. If we do a bad job, lots of people suffer. If we do a great job, who knows how many lives will be made better? That perspective makes a job like writing content or reviewing analytics feel a lot more worthwhile.

ASK A BETTER QUESTION

My goal with this book is to have a positive impact on you and to help you grow your business. If you can come away with one idea that changes your business for the better, then I will have achieved my goal. I know the power of one good idea.

I also know the power of a good question. If you want better answers, you have to ask better questions:

- Who is your customer?
- What path is your customer on?
- How can you provide more value for your customers?
- How can you do it at little to no expense?
- How can you do it when the marketing landscape seems to shift underfoot on a daily basis?

This book is focused on helping you gain a deep understanding of your customers and growing your business. I'll show you how to develop an integrated omni-channel marketing strategy that will help you do just that. This coordinated approach is what's needed to prepare your business for massive growth into the future, which is already upon us.

Think of your business as a rowing crew team. Each team member might be a strong, accomplished athlete, but if each rower's movements aren't coordinated with the entire team, the boat just spins in place. In the same way, you need more than knowledge of tactics to grow your business—you need to know how they all work together.

To that end, I'll teach you how to know your target market so well that you'll think like them and anticipate their needs. When you can predict customer needs, you can deliver amazing customer experiences.

In our accelerating digital marketplace, customer experience is already critical. As technology continues to advance and our ability to gather feedback on customers becomes ever more automated, customer experience will grow even more significant. In these pages, we'll explore new perspectives, tools, and resources for asking the right questions at the right time to maximize that experience.

GET A BETTER ANSWER

This book is for people who want better answers. It's for business owners, executives, and marketing managers of both startups and established businesses who want to develop a successful marketing strategy, track the effectiveness of what they're doing, and better understand the future of digital. In the coming chapters, you'll learn what customer-centric marketing looks like now and how it's likely to change as customers acclimate to new technology. I'll share the steps you can take now to prepare yourself to maximize that future potential.

The book is not for people who want to put their heads in the sand and just do things the way they've always done them (and keep getting the same results). It's for people who see opportunity in understanding what's coming, being able to anticipate it, and taking action now. It's for people who realize that swinging at the ball after it has been thrown means you've already missed. The ball is moving too fast. It's the same with the evolution of digital marketing: the changes are coming fast and furious, so you have to start your swing before the ball even leaves the pitcher's hand. Otherwise, you'll be swinging at air.

In part 1, we will explore the current state of marketing and digital marketing and develop a customer-centric approach that will help you succeed across channels. In part 2, we will consider key trends in artificial intelligence (AI) development that will help you prepare for the coming shift. We will also consider key trends in marketing being accelerated by AI. We'll explore the macro trends that I call the Three Ps that will be dramatically more Personalized, Predictive, and Proactive than in the past. We'll close with a consideration of how to create a customer-centric strategy with new AI, and provide some tools to get you started.

As I asked at the beginning: Are you ready? I hope you are, because change is coming whether you're ready or not. My goal is to make sure you are ready and equipped with the tools and strategy to *Future Proof Your Marketing* and to survive and thrive in the new digital arena.

PART I

THE
CURRENT
MARKETING
LANDSCAPE

CHAPTER ONE

YOU ARE HERE

GETTING THE LAY OF THE LAND

Let's begin by looking at the marketing landscape that exists today. We'll examine two apparently contradictory trends that affect every move we make in digital marketing: fragmentation and consolidation.

FRAGMENTATION

In the last ten years, we've gone from having around 200 different digital marketing tools at our disposal to being able to choose from more than 8,000. This is a reflection of the growth of digital marketing as well as the expansion of tactics and choices at our fingertips.

If you have a big enough computer screen or are prepared to paper your office walls, take a look at this: 2018 Marketing Technology Landscape Supergraphic.[1] Shared by Scott Brinker at the annual MarTech conference, this jam-packed image offers a visual representation of the number of unique marketing technology vendors offering those tools. Brinker has been assembling the supergraphic since 2011, and the 2018 number is higher than 2011 to 2016 combined!

Think about all the tools, tactics, and channels at your disposal today: different device types, the Internet of Things (IoT), search engines, social media, email, chatbots, push messaging, text, conversion rate optimization, analytics, search engine optimization, pay per click, video, and your website, just to name a few. All of these tools are available on a variety of platforms as well.

This fragmented world is full of opportunity. It allows you to efficiently target specific demographics and psychographics. If you're trying to reach customers from age twelve to twenty-four, for instance, you'll get a lot of value from being on Snapchat but probably don't need to make Facebook your number one priority. You may even want to establish yourself on an up-and-coming social entertainment network like TikTok (60 percent of its users are between sixteen and twenty-four). On the other hand, if

---

1   https://cdn.chiefmartec.com/wp-content/uploads/2018/04/marketing_technology_
landscape_2018_slide.jpg

you want to be seen by eighteen-to-forty-four-year-olds, Facebook it is.

You can also target your audience with surgical precision. New, hyperlocal platforms pop up every day. If you can get in there when the competition is light, you can grab a piece of that market. I was on Nextdoor for a while, where neighbors often communicate with each other about a number of things, including services they need and service providers. If you're a local home service provider like a plumber or handyman, this is a great way to really capture your local neighborhood. Of course, they also launched the ability to create sponsored ads, so you could test that as well, assuming you know how to track its effectiveness.

Even Google, a company that built its reputation on comprehensive search results, is getting into these niche markets with local service ads. These are call-only ads for specific service providers in specific places—plumbers, garage door contractors, locksmiths, and fence installers who live and work nearby—all vetted and guaranteed by Google. This makes it easy for the customer since they don't have to get references or do background checks. The truly brilliant thing Google is doing is hooking this local services option up to their digital assistant. If you say, "Okay, Google, help me find a plumber," it will pull up a list of people you can call directly through the assistant. If a plumber is on that list, good for them. If they aren't, they've missed a big opportunity.

NAVIGATING FRAGMENTATION

Harnessing that opportunity requires today's marketers to acknowledge that their role has changed quickly and dramatically. Fifteen to twenty years ago, an SEO marketer was responsible for areas such as keyword targeting, on-page optimization, site crawlability, and maybe some social media outreach. One person could handle that for a small company.

By 2011, however, the list had grown significantly more challenging. As Rand Fishkin says, the job of "SEO" got upgraded to "organic web strategist," with additional responsibilities including local maps optimization, reputation tracking, analytics, social media promotion, content creation, new search protocols, and new search verticals—a full plate, for sure.

As complex as the SEO role was in 2011, it was still possible for one person to manage the responsibilities for a small company by themselves. Not so today, when Google makes hundreds of changes to their algorithm every year; even specialists have to know what's going on in all of the other channels and anticipate what's coming next. No longer can you say you're just going to focus on organic search. What about remarketing campaigns, Facebook paid campaigns, Google Display, and Instagram? Did you know that Google is experimenting with a comments feature directly in their search results for sports games? Is that still search, or is it social? How can you harness that?

You need deep expertise to navigate the fragmented digital marketing world, yet you're probably behaving more like a generalist. That makes sense; you need to be aware of all the different possibilities for creating and distributing valuable content. Only then can you put together an effective plan for creation, publication, management, and promotion of all of that content.

So you need to be a specialist *and* a generalist. Tired yet?

I feel for marketers and business owners in the current landscape, because although the opportunities are plentiful, there is simply too much going on for any one person to handle alone. At the very least, you need to know enough to be able to prioritize. To truly succeed, you will probably need help from someone with deep expertise. We discovered this truth at Webfor: we started out hiring generalists but found that bringing on people who specialized in certain areas actually allowed us to be more effective. As a team, we have broad knowledge, but each team member brings a deep, up-to-the-minute knowledge in a specific area.

CONSOLIDATION

Paradoxically, as the marketing landscape gets more fragmented, some of the bigger players have bought up big chunks of that land and built consolidated marketplaces— virtual campuses that users enter and never have to leave.

The most obvious example of consolidation is probably Amazon. Remember when Amazon was just an online bookstore? Maybe you don't; it didn't last long. Today, Amazon is the starting point for nearly 50 percent of product searches done online. They purchased Whole Foods, so you can buy everything from avocados to zucchinis on Amazon, and soon, they may be delivered to your front door by drone. Why would you go anywhere else?

Everybody wants to capture as much of the traffic from as many places as they can. Consider Facebook, the largest social media platform in the world; their audience is huge—over 2 billion users as I write—but Facebook is not content to own only the social space. They also have a search capability and a messaging feature, they host events and entertainment options, and they recently launched Portal, a direct channel for people to make video calls through Facebook. The more time a user spends on their platform, the greater market share Facebook captures.

Similarly, Google, the most popular search engine in the world, is branching out into territory usually occupied by social media. As their search engine becomes more tuned in to user intent and less focused on isolated keywords, Google will begin to roll out new features like the commenting within search results that I mentioned above. When that happens, marketers want to be there, because that's where the customers will be.

Because owning vast amounts of virtual real estate is so valuable, companies are vying for control of the prime locations. They don't always succeed. Facebook hasn't actually managed to capture much search traffic, and Google's early foray into social (GooglePlus, anyone?) didn't succeed as a social media platform. That doesn't mean they're done trying, though.

Setting up your marketing "shop" in a consolidated landscape does come with risks. Even Google and Facebook can be disrupted. Working in a consolidated space is a little like building a house on someone else's land—you don't have control over what happens to the ground you built it on. The landowners might decide to make the property less valuable, as Facebook effectively did when it decreased the reach of organic posts, a space where many had staked their claim only to find it becoming less and less influential. Don't get me wrong—you need to be on Facebook and Instagram if that makes sense for your business; just don't let it be your *only* investment.

I reached out to a colleague, Rand Fishkin, founder of Moz and SparkToro (a search engine for audience intelligence), to get his thoughts on the long-term future of digital marketing. He said, "As dollars and advertisers flood the major platforms (right now, that's the Google, Amazon, Facebook tri-opoly), the ROI of throwing money at those platforms will diminish to an infinitesimally small number. Most brands will find their return at zero or even negative, and smart marketing teams will look for alternative ways to reach their audiences in the places where they pay attention. I believe that by innovating early and seeking alternative opportunities now and in the years ahead, a great marketer can stand out from their competitors and have a uniquely powerful impact."

While I don't completely agree with Rand's opinion, I think it highlights the need to have a strategy with a diversified approach and continually measure your results so you can adapt as audiences and platforms change.

NAVIGATING CONSOLIDATION

On the other hand, the "captive audiences" that enter a

consolidated space and rarely leave it represents a huge opportunity for marketers.

Let me give you a brief glimpse into the future. One of the biggest opportunities in the lifetime of the big tech companies is fast approaching, and they all know it: they are all fighting to capture the digital personal assistant market. Amazon has Alexa, Apple has Siri, Google has Google Assistant, Microsoft has Cortana, and Will.i.am has Omega. Yes, you heard that correctly. Will.i.am, the rapper/singer/entrepreneur recently debuted his AI-powered digital assistant called Omega. Honestly, when huge innovations happen, disruption can occur; he has 300 employees working on this, and Salesforce Ventures backed his company with a $117 million-dollar investment. I'm excited to see what he comes up with!

So why am I talking about this related to consolidation? Well, you've probably heard the term "gatekeeper" when talking about a person's executive assistant. This is because a really good assistant is going to know you—they're going to understand what's important to you and know your schedule. They're going to proactively handle things for you based on their knowledge and the rules you set forth. They will make decisions on your behalf, and free you up to focus on real high-priority items.

As these tech companies race to see who can create the

best virtual personal assistant, they will continually make advancements, and these digital assistants will likely act as the gateway between the individual and many of their activities, just like a real assistant would. They might take some of your calls for you, remind you of upcoming meetings, purchase something on your behalf, search for the best restaurant to have lunch, and even respond to your emails. **It's very possible that these digital assistants could become the largest gateway to all other marketing channels.**

Most assistants are built on the same data that search engines use, which is why companies that have extensive knowledge bases, such as Google and Microsoft, are poised to take advantage of the changes to come. As these companies collect an astounding amount of data, index and categorize it, they position themselves as authoritative sources by returning only the best answers. They're the librarians, or trusted knowledge keepers, of the digital world.

As digital assistants become the gateway to the consolidated campus, you need to make sure you're standing by at the port of entry, because users will no longer be scrolling through search results to find your name, even if it surfaces on the coveted first page of results. Instead, when your potential customer asks a question, they may receive only one answer—the "best" answer—in reply. If your customer starts every query by saying, "Hey, Alexa," you want to be the answer Alexa gives.

While there's a lot more to it, the base idea is to gain a deep understanding of your customers and their journey around your product or service. You want to know the questions they ask, their needs, and their concerns, and then create massive value by addressing these in a meaningful way during each step in their journey. Creating in-depth content around these topics will help establish your expertise as an authoritative and trusted source. When you do this, search engines will surface that information to potential customers because they believe you will provide them with value and satisfy their need.

CHAPTER TWO

WHO'S WITH YOU?

GETTING TO KNOW YOUR CUSTOMER

If you want to be the answer your customer gets, you need to understand who that customer is. Common sense, you say? Maybe, but many company founders start out with a passion for a product or a process but not a lot of focus on the customer. Their passion can carry them for a while, but eventually, most business owners have to shift that focus or find someone to help them do that.

For instance, one international touring company we recently met with was founded on that kind of passion. The founder's father taught German and, as he neared retirement, began taking people on walking tours of Germany. He was passionate about introducing people to other cultures, his clients loved him, and pretty soon he was branching out into other countries.

As the family business grew and was passed on to the son, they tried a number of tactics to reach customers online. They ran some paid campaigns through Google AdWords. They tried Facebook. They tried to create content to capture organic search traffic. These were all good ideas, but they lacked a cohesive strategy and focus on the customer.

We walked them through how to get into their customers' heads and understand their journey, or in other words, what they are feeling, thinking, and doing as they interact across multiple channels and move through different stages of the buying process. We also showed them a number of technical problems they were creating. By doing a few simple things, they could leverage content they already had and reach many more customers with very little financial investment. The real investment was in their mindset—they had to shift from just focusing on the product to focusing on the person who would use the product.

CUSTOMER-CENTRIC MARKETING

Everything we do needs to be focused on understanding the customer across multiple stages of the customer journey. To understand how powerful that focus can be, consider Zappos. Zappos knows how important it is to create a great customer experience, and they have developed a corporate culture that encourages and supports their employees to serve the customers what they need and want.

Founded by Nick Swinmurn in 2006, Zappos started with an unusual idea—selling shoes online. Who would buy shoes online, where you couldn't try them on? It turned out that lots of people would. Some people were already buying shoes that way—about 5 percent of sales in the $40 billion market was already being done through catalogs or mail order.

To take advantage of the apparent opportunity, Zappos had to do things differently. They didn't rely on technology for that but on what they understood about the psychology behind the customer experience. Something was holding other people back from buying shoes online. What was it? Could they fix it? They realized that one big reason customers were hesitant was that they disliked the uncertainty of buying shoes they had never seen in person, touched, tried on, and experienced. Would the shoes even fit? How could customers be sure they would get what they needed?

By now, most people know the answer, because Zappos is well known for its no-question, no-cost return policy. You can buy six pairs of shoes, keep the ones you want, and send the others back anytime within a year, no matter the reason. If you're not happy with them, back they go. This gives customers a sense of certainty that makes them much more comfortable with buying online.

THE PLEASURE PRINCIPLE

Zappos understood an essential truth: that people tend to gravitate toward things that they believe will make them happy or bring them pleasure, and away from things that they associate with pain or discomfort. Sigmund Freud called this basic human instinct the "pleasure principle." Your customer is no different. If you provide a pleasurable, pain-free experience, they will seek you out and stay with you.

Most people are drawn to experiences that provide a sense of certainty, significance, impact, and belonging. That's why Zappos decided to remove all of the uncertainty from the online shoe-buying process. They also made sure the customer felt important by treating everyone with respect, no matter their request or complaint. Zappos's customers can also feel good about working with the company, because it's known for its animal advocacy and environmental programs. Finally, with so many people saying great things about Zappos online, customers can feel that they're part of the greater community.

On the other end of the spectrum, people are generally primed to try and avoid pain; our reptilian brain helps us by making sure we fight against, or flee, from anything that threatens our ability to survive. We don't get a lot of practice fighting off man-eating tigers in the modern world, yet the pain-avoidance instinct remains, leading us to react similarly to any threat of loss.

This is valuable knowledge for marketers. If you don't want people to flee from your efforts, make them feel safe. If you want to attract them, fulfill their desires. Easy, right? The trick is, different people associate different things with pain and pleasure. Some people love broccoli; others hate it. Likewise, some people will be put off by having to fill out a three-page form on your website and run away as fast as they can, while others who feel that anything worth having is worth working for will gladly roll up their sleeves and dig in. That's why you have to know *your* particular customer really, really well—so you can align your efforts with their preferences.

Too often, people make assumptions about their customers without putting themselves in the customer's shoes. I call this "Brand Blindness." We worked with a company like this—a successful coffee shop chain with about thirty locations. Even though they had locations in multiple cities, they rarely showed up on the first page of search results when people searched for coffee shops in those cities. They thought they should be focusing on only social media and told us that search engines didn't matter to them, because "everyone knows who we are." However, when we looked into it, we discovered that the number of searches in their city for their brand were minuscule compared to the 20,000 searches a month for the general term "coffee shops."

We showed them that quite often, convenience trumps brand loyalty in their industry, and they had two huge opportunities if they showed up in these 20,000+ searches a month. One was to capture a new audience and create new, loyal customers. The other was to prevent their *current* loyal customers from getting a taste of other great brands. If they have a high brand affinity and you show up when they search, they may drive a little farther to get to your coffee shop.

The reason wasn't any of the things this company was looking at, like brand loyalty. It was much simpler—convenience. There was this large audience of potential customers that were searching for what they offered every month, but they wanted to quickly and easily find a cool coffee shop close by, with free Wi-Fi. That was it. When this shop didn't appear in local search results, let alone advertise its Wi-Fi availability, the company missed out on customers who would have been thrilled to find them.

FUDD

Many business owners, like the coffee shop owner, make plans based on how they feel, think, and act—not on how the *customer* feels, thinks, and acts. That's unfortunate, because to effectively and efficiently reach your unique customer, you need to understand who that person is and how they relate to your specific business. I often use the acronym FUDD to describe some of the ways customers are unique—you need to understand their Fears, Uncertainties, Desires, and Decision-Making processes.

Every business is different, and so is every customer. A person looking for a restaurant will have very different fears, uncertainties, and desires than someone looking for a hospice facility for their mother who has cancer. The stages of their customer journey will unfold in very different ways, and nobody likes being offered a "one-size-fits-all" solution, because that promise is usually hollow. When you tailor your approach instead, you can meet their needs better than anyone else.

Do your clients tend to be careful, methodical rule-followers? Or are they risk-takers, likely to be early adopters of anything new that comes along? Are they visual processors or word people? If you know that, you can tailor your messaging to better resonate with them. Just changing a few words in your campaigns can make a huge difference in who you reach and how effectively you reach them.

TALK IT OUT

Most of us have blind spots about our customers. We make assumptions. The thing is, there's an easy solution. Allow me to share a cutting-edge technique most people aren't using:

Talk to them.

Sure, it sounds obvious now that I say it, but many people overlook this option. I know how it is—it can be easy to overlook the most important pieces of the puzzle when you're looking right at them, because you aren't seeing what's there. Talking to your customer is honestly one of the easiest and most effective ways to find out who they really are, and I encourage you to do it!

To get started, you can make a list of three of your best customers. These will be people you love working with and who give you a lot of business. Then invite them out to lunch or ask if you can jump on a phone call with them. Tell them they're one of your best customers, you love working with them, and you want to make their experience—and the experience of other customers—even better. Let them know they can help by entertaining a few of your questions.

Then sit down with them and focus on their needs. The questions you ask depend on the kind of business you run, so you'll want to tailor them to your industry, but they should be aimed at understanding the customer journey from the earliest stages:

- What made them aware they needed your product or service?
- What problem were they trying to solve?
- What methods did they use to try to solve it? Did they ask their friends? See an ad? Use a search engine?
- What were they feeling throughout the process? Frustrations? Fears?
- What thoughts were going through their mind? Costs? Value? Return policy?
- What technology did they use? Mobile phone? Desktop computer?
- What was their most desired outcome?
- What ultimately prompted them to take action?
- Why did they choose you?
- How could you make the experience better for them?

These conversations deepen the relationship with the customer and provide valuable feedback you can use with other customers. When their feedback helps you see and solve a problem, follow up with them to let them know. Share how you smoothed out that snag in the onboarding process because of them.

In some cases, you may not have direct access to the

customer. If that's your situation, the next best step is talking to people on the front line of your business—the salespeople and customer service people who know your customers best. (You should do this anyway to get additional insights into the customer experience.) Chances are, they can tell you the parts of the customer journey that delight people and the parts that frustrate them, because they interact with them every day. They probably know the patterns already, but if they don't, one easy way to find out is to provide a simple spreadsheet of questions to the person answering the phone or emails; every time a customer asks a question, they make a hash mark. If it's a new question, they write it down. Pretty soon you will see patterns, like customers regularly calling in a panic about price and needing to be calmed down before they will take action. This might indicate that your website messaging gives the wrong impression about price, and you can fix that.

PERSONAS

There's no substitute for talking with your customer face-to-face, but that's not always possible for everyone in your organization. Developing customer personas can help you get this in-depth customer knowledge in front of everyone so your content writers to your customer service personnel can better connect with your customers.

Personas are composite portraits of your customer that allow you to tailor your communications to meet them where they are. Broad personas are general categories. "Top Dog Tom" might be the CEO, while "Marketing Manager Mary" is a marketing executive, for example. There is some value in these personas—they give team members a way to communicate about the audience in a general way—but the real treasure lies in detailed personas.

A detailed persona is an extremely specific "character," or avatar. He or she has a name, a backstory, certain fears, uncertainties, desires, and decision-making preferences. Your persona's attributes might include the types of devices they use, what they want to achieve, what they hate, and what they love. You can get surprisingly detailed—do they like to drink wine? Do they go to the opera? Snowboard? All of this converges in one document along with demographic details like age and home ownership. We've created a simple Word document that you can use to start building your first persona along with some of the other tools I will share. You can download it here: Webfor.com/ideal-customer.

BUILDING A CUSTOMER-CENTRIC CULTURE

Individual tools like personas are powerful; they can help you understand your customer better than ever. Perhaps even more important, though, is building a company culture that supports this customer-centric philosophy. As we've seen, Zappos is a legend in the customer service arena, and much of their success stems from their corporate culture.

Zappos's customer service folks really are there to help, and there's a popular story about Zappos's CEO Tony Hsieh and friends using Zappos to get a pizza. As the story goes, they were up late after a conference and couldn't find a place to deliver a pizza to the hotel room. What could be done? Maybe they should call Zappos! A real person answered the call, regardless of the time. She may have been a bit surprised to hear a pizza order coming down the line, but she rallied. She listened to the caller's predicament—2:30 a.m. and no pizza delivery to be found—and asked him to hang on for a minute. When she came back, she had located three pizza places in the area. She took the caller's credit card, ordered the pizza, and had it delivered.

This moment was exceptional, but Zappos's customer service people behave differently than most on an everyday basis. For instance, while most call centers try to limit the time each agent spends on the phone—shorter calls mean they can service more people—Zappos actually rewards their people for long calls. There are prizes for the longest time spent on the phone. Legend has it that the record was a ten-hour call!

Zappos is so good at customer service that other companies seek them out and want to learn from them. In response, they've started a program called Zappos Insights, where they teach other companies about culture and customer experience.

As I said at the beginning of this book, I believe customer experience is going to become one of the largest ranking factors in the next five to ten years. As technology advances, companies will put a much higher priority on customer experience. They might be doing some of it now—we all want our customers to have a great experience—but in the future, it will make or break the business. The good news is that the new technology will greatly increase our ability to understand who our customers are, where they are, and what they're doing so we can meet them there.

CHAPTER THREE

WHAT PEOPLE ARE DOING

UNCOVERING YOUR CUSTOMERS' JOURNEY

The customer journey is constantly evolving, fragmented, and may not follow a common path. Customers conduct research through the use of various devices and are active in numerous different channels. It is a growing challenge to meet customers where they're at and deliver exceptional experiences that meet their high expectations. The crucial first step is diving in and gaining an in-depth understanding of your customers' journey.

To get to know your customer, you have to learn how they behave: what they are doing, where they are doing it, and with whom. Do you know what communities your customer interacts with? What are the common stops along the path to purchase your product or service? If you know your customer and you know the path they take, don't you think it will be a lot easier to get the right message in front of them at the right time? Of course it would!

Before we dive in and give you the tools and tactics to uncover your customers' journey, I want you to have a solid understanding of the different marketing channels, common tactics, and how they all work together. I'm going to provide you with some visualizations to provide context on how to best develop a customer-centric digital marketing strategy. As you can see in the image, your customer is at the center of your strategy.

When you create a customer-centric digital strategy, you must focus all of your activity around the customer.

That's your bullseye, the target you created by talking to customers, creating personas, and so on. To serve them, you need to understand their behaviors, actions, thoughts, and feelings across multiple stages of the customer journey.

You also need to consider the people who may not be your customers but are going to help elevate your brand and get you in front of more potential customers. Your digital strategy must include efforts to engage these endorsers. They will differ for each business, but endorsers can include strategic partners, media, publishers, competitors and peers (in some industries), suppliers, thought leaders, and influencers who have a positive opinion of you, your product, or your service. They might mention you in a story they write, link to your website, offer testimonials, write reviews, share your content on social media, or even partner with you in content creation.

You also want to think about your presence in the community. This includes how you want to be perceived, how you want to be involved, how you will give back, and the people and/or organizations whom you want to be connected with. This is a large group and includes everybody who interacts with you in any manner, whether it's through your website, email, social media, search, or in person. Community is a big component to building your company culture as well as developing true brand affinity, which will ultimately make your strategy much more effective.

In this chapter, we'll focus on the main broad channels people use—search, social, and direct. I like to explain these as consumer behaviors that overlap quite nicely with the corresponding marketing channels. As you can see in the visual, the different channels overlap and benefit each other when they work together in an integrated strategy.

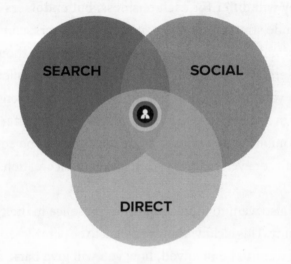

SEARCH

The search channel covers everything a person does when they're searching for something on the web. They might be browsing, asking questions, initiating searches, or just looking up a company name. The search channel includes all of the search engines as well as the network of sites they display their ads on. It combines organic search engine results generated by the search engine's algorithms (earned media) as well as paid ad campaigns (paid media).

Search is generally an excellent channel for business because many consumers start their buying process with search. Consumers have more access to information now than ever before, and the average consumer references twelve sources before making a purchase.[2] They perform numerous searches, visit websites, compare products, and read reviews. As a business, you have to make sure you effectively manage your presence online so you not only show up prominently in the main places they go, but you also offer clear value. You can't just hope that happens—you have to have a strategy.

If you want to be found, it helps to understand the patterns people tend to follow when they search. As a general rule, the more complex the decision and the larger the purchase, the bigger the role of the search channel. If someone is going to build a home, for example, they'll probably do a lot of initial research online. They'll spend a significant amount of time reading about the process

2   Beth Thomas, Erin Dean, Kelly Smith, Nina Thatcher, "Holiday Is (Almost)
     Here: 5 Shopping Trends Marketers Should Watch in 2014," thinkwithgoogle.
     com, August 2014, https://www.thinkwithgoogle.com/consumer-insights/
     five-holiday-shopping-trends-marketers-should-watch/.

and perusing home builders' websites—much more time than they'd spend looking for a convenience store down the street. In other, more urgent situations—say they've got a burst water pipe—people will spend even less time searching. They just want to find someone, anyone, who will help them now!

Either way, you want to show up on the first page of search results, high on the page, because otherwise, it's like the old joke: "Where do you hide a dead body? The second page of Google, because nobody goes there!" To place higher, you can implement a search engine optimization strategy and create high-quality content that search engines deem highly valuable for your targeted topics and rank it in their top organic results. You can also develop a paid ad campaign to put you front and center with a variety of different ad types at different stages in the customer journey.

Although it's rare, there are some quick fixes that can have an enormous impact. We worked with a global IT company that was missing out on millions of dollars in opportunity because of one simple problem. They had an old, inactive website that had thousands of links pointing to it from other highly authoritative sites, such as Stanford University, but it wasn't being properly redirected to their new site.

Search engines look at the links to your website like

endorsements or votes, and getting a link from Stanford would be like getting an electoral vote—it would carry a lot of weight and authority, and the IT company was missing out on that association. We were able to reclaim a number of these high-value links for them and move them to the first page of search results for a number of their high-value keyword phrases. This one change can mean millions of dollars a year for a company like this.

Another company we worked with had purchased their largest competitor and wanted our help to integrate the content and redirect 2.3 million URLs on that site over to their own. Normally, in a project like this, your goal is to reduce any potential loss in traffic as there usually will be some. In this case, they saw over a 400 percent increase in traffic. That drove huge growth and revenue for this company.

Search engines are looking to provide their customers with the best assistance along their path. This may be providing a quick answer or suggesting resources to review. Companies with a strong foundation in search recognize this; they develop their expertise in a specific topic or category, they build their authority as a domain, as an individual, and as a brand, and they work to earn the public trust. In other words, if you provide content hubs with excellent value and SEO best practices in mind, search engines will send customers your way.

This value comes in the form of content like images, text, video, audio, interactive experiences, and a number of other resources that range from educational to entertaining. Unfortunately, as much as 90 percent of companies aren't consistently creating high-quality content, and those that are creating content often don't understand what the user is looking for. If you can get into the customer's head and understand how they use search, you can maximize your content so it reaches them.

Search should be a primary channel for your business if you know that lots of people are looking for what you offer. If the demand is clear, then you should make search a focus of your digital strategy. There's a good chance that people are out there searching for information related to your product or service every day. If you make sure you're in front of these searchers at the right time, you are going to get a high return on your investment.

If, on the other hand, fewer people are searching on topics related to your product, search might make up a smaller part of your efforts, or you might need to create awareness before investing heavily in search. Some customers come to us seeking search engine optimization (SEO) help, when the reality is, they have just launched a brand-new product nobody has heard of that solves a problem nobody is yet seeking a solution for. There just isn't enough search volume to make SEO useful for them right away. We encourage them to utilize other channels to start getting in front of their audience, such as paid media campaigns and social media.

SOCIAL

The social channel includes any place where people are interacting socially. Social includes in-person meetings and phone calls, as well as social media platforms such as Facebook, Instagram, Twitter, or Pinterest.

Just like search, social has earned media and paid media. Organic reach (earned media) on popular platforms like Facebook has decreased significantly over the last few years to the point where many brands are turning much of their focus toward paid media campaigns. This doesn't mean you should completely abandon organic social strategies, but it can mean that you may need to "grease the wheel" a little by boosting some of your content to start building engagement.

Social media allows you to harness the power of fragmentation. Niche communities thrive here, so the more specialized your product or service, the more niche your audience, the higher the probability that social will work for you. If you have a niche audience, social could be a great way to reach them. Even if you have a broad audience, you can segment your audience into hyper-specific niches.

I once worked with a new business with a unique audience: speech therapists. The company was launching a website where speech therapists could upload and sell their materials and exercises for other therapists to use in their work. We were able to create a campaign that targeted women between the ages of twenty-six and fifty who graduated with a degree in speech pathology and were working as speech therapists. Because the audience was so niche, we were able to target the whole United States at a very favorable cost per conversion. We drove a number of people to sign up prior to the launch of the website, at very low cost. Because we were able to target the audience so clearly, our messaging could be very specific, with a good hook tailored to the people we wanted to reach.

Online or in real life, the more social your business is, the better the social channel will perform for you. If your product is something people don't want to talk about publicly—adult diapers, for example—you're not going to get much traction here. If, on the other hand, you run a restaurant, you'll generate lots of social media buzz—digital "word of mouth" works wonders. Believe it or not, all of those posts featuring pictures of people's food are incredibly valuable.

GETTING CREATIVE

These are general "rules of thumb" when it comes to advertising on social, but I always say thumbs are meant to be broken! Please take what I've said with a grain of salt—there are always exceptions to the rule.

For example, I once had someone challenge me by saying, "Well, there's no way you're going to get adults to share content around adult diapers," to which I replied, "You're 99 percent correct, but let's explore the remaining 1 percent." I believe that even a brand that isn't ideal for social can get creative once in a while, assuming it fits their brand, so I took this comment as a challenge. Yes, I created an ad campaign for adult diapers. Here's what I came up with.

Two guys are watching a football game, and both of them have a beer in hand. The text overlays along with the audio, "You've been drinking...A LOT! You REALLY have to go to the bathroom, but the score is tied, there's thirty seconds left in the game and your team's about to score. What do you do?

[The logo fades in...] "Depends"

While this may or may not work with Depends's brand identity, I guarantee this would get a tremendous number of shares, especially if it was released around the time of the Super Bowl.

Any business that depends on frequent repurchases, like restaurants, will find the social channel beneficial. If you have a consumable product and you want people to come back over and over again, you want to stay in touch with them. Social media makes that easy. Put your "Taco Tuesday" special on your Facebook page and keep the customer engaged. That way, you keep them coming back and provide an opportunity for them to share information about you with others on their social networks. You might also provide opportunities here for your best customers to join an even more elite club—the direct channel, where you can deepen the relationship even more.

DIRECT

The direct channel is when you and/or your customer start communicating directly with each other. You may be utilizing email, text messages, phone calls, automation, CRMs, chatbots, or even push notifications to do this. While social and search tend to be the drivers of new potential customers, the direct channel tends to facilitate communication and drive them further down the funnel to take action and make a purchase.

There are few things you own in your marketing strategy, but along with your website, your customers' contact information should be a high priority for you. Platforms can lessen their reach or go out of business, so while you should definitely focus on earned and paid media, you want to make sure you understand what you actually own.

The direct channel is valuable because it helps customers at a variety of points in the buying process. In the early stages, they might be looking for information on your website. You can harness that by offering valuable information—"Seven Things You Must Know Before Buying Your First Home"—that they can download. You could collect their email in this process to be able to send additional valuable content (with their permission of course).

People may be seeking more information, considering a purchase, requesting a consultation, or seeking an estimate. They begin a relationship with you when they fill out a form on your website, send you an email, or start a chat with you. Even if they're just signing up for your newsletter, this interaction offers an opportunity to deepen your connection with them. A simple newsletter subscription can make them feel a part of your community, which is the first step toward becoming a customer. To bring them in even further, you might offer a loyalty points program or other rewards.

When they sign up for your email, they may be just dipping their toe in the water as far as becoming part of your community, but if you stay top of mind and continue to provide exceptional value, they're more likely to dive into the deep end. If you run a drip campaign to deliver one of those seven tips each day, you put yourself in front of them seven days in a row. Later on, they might request a consultation or inquire about an estimate. In all of these scenarios, their engagement offers an opportunity for you to deepen your relationship with them and bring them further down the funnel.

BETTER ENGAGEMENT WITH CHATBOTS

Chatbots are one of the new technologies/tools/tactics that fall into this channel. Chatbots can be extremely helpful and reduce overhead by carrying on conversations with multiple customers at the same time. They can handle everything from answering customer support questions to assisting with lead generation.

I reached out to a colleague, Larry Kim, Founder of Mobile Monkey and developer of a chatbot that works with the Facebook Messenger platform, to find out what he thought about the expansion of this technology. He said, "I've seen ten to eighty times better engagement through Facebook Messenger blasts than I have with traditional email campaigns or organic social posts." Those statistics are amazing!

Because you're developing a relationship with the customer, you need to be careful about how you communicate with them. Consider whether your efforts might be experienced as intrusive. Facebook Messenger could be a great tactic to grow your audience and drive more leads, but if your audience sees those messages as invasive, you've shot yourself in the foot. You might start with a small test audience to see how a new tactic or technology is received.

Many businesses fail to look at this issue from the customer's perspective. Choose the method that works best for *them*, not you. I have seen many companies offer customer support only by email simply because it's easiest for them. Honestly, your comfort is not what's important.

You need to make it easy for your customer. Remember, your ultimate goal is not just to get a customer but a customer who will sing your praises and bring you even more customers. I call those customers "brand champions." To do that, you have to provide value throughout the entire customer experience.

OTHER CHANNELS

I encourage every business to develop their search, social, and direct channels, because those channels offer the most value to the most people. With certain clients, I also recommend considering other channels, like gaming and entertainment. There is still a place for traditional media as well, including traditional broadcast media. For instance, TV or radio campaigns can build awareness and drive your customer to take action—maybe it sends them to your website to learn more. You're bringing them into the digital funnel. As always, it depends on what your business does and what your customers want.

CROSSING CHANNELS

The ultimate goal is to create an integrated strategy that takes all, or at least most, of the available channels into consideration. Creating such an omni-channel strategy can be challenging. On the other hand, having such a strategy offers incredible opportunity because your message reverberates across the channels and reaches more people.

Say your customer finds some valuable content on your website through their search efforts. That's fantastic, but you can do more to drive them further down the funnel. When they decide to download that content, they may sign up for your newsletter. When you send them that first email, you're reaching them directly. If you include an invitation to your Facebook page, you send them to the social channel, where they can click "Like" and move others to take action.

Each channel benefits the others, not only to move the original customer along the buying journey but also to motivate new customers to take action. When you have a cohesive strategy, each channel works together, and the positive interactions the customer has in each channel is like gravity pulling them closer into your community; they might possibly become an endorser and then a customer. If your new customer has a great experience, they may share it on social media, refer you to friends and colleagues, or leave you a positive review. Now your new customer has become a brand champion and is out there doing marketing for you.

For example, social media can be a great place to build your community. When you create highly valuable, entertaining, educational, useful content, your audience is more likely to share it. When they do that, there are more eyeballs on your content. There's also a higher chance that one of those "endorsers" might mention you or link to you. This will also benefit your presence in the search channel. The key to harnessing the power of these channels is to leverage that overlap. Your brand needs to be represented in the main arenas your customer might encounter you, and your messaging must be cohesive and engaging as it's distributed across the channels.

WHAT ARE YOUR USERS DOING?

Clearly, search, social, and direct channels are all important, but how do you allocate your resources? Start by keeping your goal firmly in mind: You want to be clearly present and visible to your customers as much as possible and drive the desired interactions. You could have the best content in the world, but if they don't see it, they don't see *you*.

You will want to prioritize your channel mix based on all of your research. If your research shows that search is your first priority, social is second, and direct is third, then your channel prioritization may look like this image.

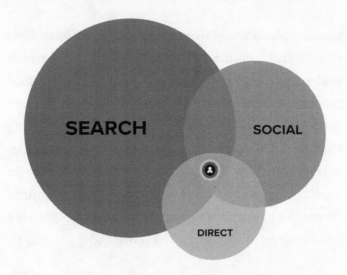

However, if social is your first priority, direct is second, and search is third, it might look like this.

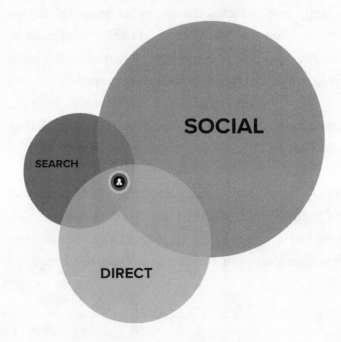

This was essentially the problem an auto body shop brought to us at Webfor. One issue was that search should have been a huge draw for them—plenty of people in the area were searching for "auto body shop" and "collision repair," but they weren't appearing in the search results. I discovered one of the main problems when I tried to navigate the company's website from my mobile phone.

First, the site loaded slowly and that caused people to give up (after about three seconds, 53 percent of people on a mobile phone will abandon a site).[3] Second, the site was not optimized for mobile, so even if someone did wait for it to load, they couldn't possibly read the teeny tiny text that eventually emerged. Not surprisingly, the shop was losing customers. Nobody standing on the side of the road with a damaged car is going to spend time trying to navigate that. They're going to move on to the next shop on the list.

Social could have been a useful channel for the auto body shop, too, but they were doing almost nothing on that end. It was much the same in the direct channel—they didn't have a newsletter or any email outreach to stay in touch with their customers or strategic partners. This shop was operating like a boxer heading into a match with only one jab at his disposal—they had a good reputation

---

3   Jason Cohen, "Why Mobile Page Speed Is a Visual Designer's Problem," thinkwithgoogle. com, March 2017, https://www.thinkwithgoogle.com/intl/en-cee/insights-trends/ux-design/ why-mobile-page-speed-visual-designers-problem/.

which gave them an edge but not enough to sustain them throughout the match.

We worked with them to create a comprehensive strategy that provided value to customers in each stage of the customer journey and in each of the channels. We helped them create a new website that is optimized for mobile friendliness, speed, usability, and navigation. We created hyperlocal campaigns around each of their locations, and a social media campaign that featured before-and-after pictures of cars they had fixed. We helped them create content they could use on their new site and feed to interested customers through direct channels. Almost immediately, they began seeing a big increase in conversions.

Unfortunately, this particular client hadn't been measuring their conversions prior to working with us so we can't tell you how much they improved year over year, but within the first couple of months, we saw a 22 percent increase in conversions from the first month we started. (This lack of concrete data for comparison highlights the importance of measuring the effectiveness of your marketing efforts, and we'll discuss more about that shortly.)

DIGGING FOR GOLD

So how do you know where to start? How much do you invest and where?

Let's say you're a small business with a limited budget, and you assume search is your gold mine, and you're certain social media is a dead zone for you. Are you right? Maybe you don't need to be on Snapchat, but can you afford to ignore social media entirely? Possibly, but you need to know more before you make that decision.

We all want to strike gold with our marketing efforts, but even if you have the best digging equipment available, you are probably not going to strike it rich if you just start digging in a random spot. Picking the right place to dig is crucial. You need to do solid research to narrow down your options to a few spots where gold is likely to be found. Only then should you start digging.

One of the best ways to find out where to focus your resources is to see where the other treasure hunters are digging.

COMPETITIVE ANALYSIS

To discover where at least some of the gold is, you can reverse engineer your competitors' efforts by asking some key questions:

- What is your main competitor's keyword market share?
- How is their website user experience?

- Are their emails engaging?
- Which channels are producing the most traffic or traction for them?

It's surprisingly easy to find all of this out. Tools like SimilarWeb and SEMrush (see the appendix for a more complete list) will tell you the basics, such as the company's product or service, how many employees they have, and where their headquarters are. They'll also reveal more specific information, such as how much website traffic they have, how long the average person stays on their site, and what percentage of visitors come from what countries.

Dig a little deeper and you can discover how those visitors get to the website; specifically, you can find out what percentage of traffic comes from search engines, social media, and direct marketing. If you are currently getting 1 percent of your website traffic from social media sources and you discover that your biggest competitor who gets even more traffic than you do gets 10 percent of their traffic from social, you've just learned something important about what *your* customers are probably doing online. Beyond that, you can even drill down within each category to discover how much of the competitor's search returns come from paid campaigns versus organic and even see which ad platforms they are using.

Recently, we did some competitive analysis for a client. We did a keyword market share comparison for them, which analyzes the number of keywords that their website shows up for in search engines compared to their competitors' websites. You'll see in this graphic that their competitors showed up for considerably more keywords than they did. This helped to provide context for the opportunity that was in front of them.

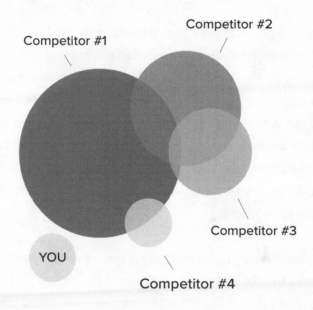

We can also uncover all of the individual keywords that their competitors are showing up for and which ones their customers are using most often. This can uncover tremendous untapped opportunity.

People are often surprised by what they find through

competitive analysis. You might assume Facebook would take the top spot in any company's social media efforts, but instead, you discover that your competitors have a ton of success with Reddit, which you've never considered. Knowing this doesn't mean you have to go out and pursue Reddit, but maybe you should check it out—is it worth getting into such a niche website, and if you do, what's the best way to approach them?

You can get incredibly granular with your analysis. One of my favorite tools, SEMrush, can tell you that Amazon shows up in search results for 76 million keywords, exactly what keywords they are, how much traffic each of those keywords gets, where Amazon is ranked for those keywords, and how competitors are ranking for those keywords. You can also discover what kinds of paid ads they run and what paid and organic keywords they're targeting.

If you reverse engineer what others are doing, you can begin to take action much closer to the source. When I explain this to marketing managers, executives, and business owners, they are blown away by how much information is available. There's a lot of gold in them thar hills!

One caveat on competitive intelligence: It can be tempting to try out every tactic you discover your successful competitors are using, but beware of "shiny object syndrome," or trying the latest tactic even though it's not really right for you. Looking at high-success tactics and best practices can be informative, but I advise against trying a single tactic in isolation.

I know it's tempting. As we saw in chapter 1, marketing teams today are overloaded with work and are often expected to do more than their expertise allows. No wonder everyone is looking for a silver bullet that can magically hit the target. Unfortunately, they're very unlikely to find it. Working the tactics together as part of a strategy that takes into account all of the channels creates a synergy where the whole is greater than the sum of its parts. You may think you don't have the resources to invest in such a cohesive strategy, but I encourage you to think about all of the opportunities you'll miss if you don't consider all of the available channels. It's time to start preparing for the new era of intelligent digital assistants that will be the facilitator of an increasingly larger share of our customer interactions.

CHAPTER FOUR

HOW TO CREATE A CUSTOMER-CENTRIC STRATEGY

PUTTING WHERE, WHO, AND WHAT TOGETHER

Beyond sleuthing your competitors' strategy, the most important thing you can do to make your marketing efforts succeed is to develop a deep level of understanding and empathy with your customers. You should know your customers well enough that you're able to predict what they need before they even need it. This is true now and will be even more true in the future.

WHAT IS A CUSTOMER-CENTRIC MARKETING STRATEGY ANYWAY?

So what is a customer-centric marketing strategy? It's a plan that focuses on your customers and aims to achieve a business objective through marketing and measurement. Although it's tempting to try every new trendy tactic that comes your way—and it's a popular way to go— people who focus on tactics instead of strategy often find themselves swimming in circles. They might be doing all of the tactics correctly, but if they don't know what direction they're heading in, they won't make meaningful progress. Instead, you need to develop a thoughtful strategy that will guide you to choose the tactics that are most likely to provide value for you. You can deploy dozens of tactics with the utmost care and precision, but if they're not part of a larger strategy, you will not be as effective.

The biggest benefit of developing a customer-centered focus is that it will inform your entire strategy. It tells you what kind of messaging to create, who needs to see it, where it should go, and when. Perhaps the most surprising benefit of understanding your customer is that it gives you an excellent communications tool, inside and outside your organization. When you bring on a new employee, you can tell them who the customer is by providing training around customers' known fears and concerns and the way your company addresses them. That gets everyone on the same page, delivering a much higher level of experience to the customer.

If you decide at some point to hire an outside marketing agency, having this strategy in place will help you communicate with them as well. You already have in-depth, documented knowledge about the customer, so you can jump right into talking strategy first and then tactics.

One of the first questions we ask businesses is what sets them apart from others in their field. Most of them give the same response: "customer service." While customer service is important, every business tells their customers this. It isn't the way to capture the hearts and minds of your customers. Instead, think about one of your favorite customer stories. How did you truly impact them and their life? Every business can say that they have great customer service, but you need to know what psychological need you're filling for your customers. **Your customers aren't buying your product or service—they're buying a better version of themselves.** So how will their lives be better with your product or service in it? What unique value do you bring to them? And are you able to communicate this in a way that resonates on a deeper level?

If you don't have a unique value proposition that truly addresses your customers' needs and distinguishes you from your competitors, you can read the following blog I wrote on the topic and download the easy-to-use Unique Value Proposition worksheet. I'd recommend doing that now.

- Unique Value Proposition blog and worksheet: Webfor.com/uvp

To be truly effective, you need to develop a deeply customer-centric marketing strategy based on understanding the customer and their entire journey. However, many businesses are still operating under old beliefs that keep them from making authentic connections. Here are four myths we hear frequently—and the reality that blows away each myth:

MYTH #1
Companies should act professionally at all times.

REALITY
Customers want you to be personable, and they feed off your passion.

To truly engage today's customers, companies will need to shed the belief that professionalism requires them to be formal and somewhat aloof. That old-fashioned belief holds a lot of businesses back. Instead, you need to approach the customer from a place of openness, authenticity, and even vulnerability. In this way, you're likely to get their attention more easily and also engage them for the long term, because they develop a sense of trust.

MYTH #2

You need to appeal to everyone.

REALITY

You need to go deep, not wide, and focus on your best customer.

You don't have to appeal to all customers—you have to decide who your customer is and fall in love with them. Get to know everything about them and overdeliver. Provide value to them in everything from your visuals to your processes to your support, such that everything is aligned with their needs. You'll bring in a bunch of other customers along the way, but your focus should be on that core customer.

At Webfor, we wrestled with the misconception of appealing to all customers, but as we grew, we came to realize that we can't be everything to everyone. We can, however, be the right solution for the customers who need us most—the people who want to grow their business and are driven to reach the next level to make that happen. We focus on bringing on clients where we can have a major impact for them. We pass on a number of projects to maintain this customer-centric focus, but it's the best for everyone in the long run. By taking on the best customer fit for us, we're more likely to deliver and help them achieve their goals.

MYTH #3

You should just focus on creating a great product.

REALITY

You must focus on people.

Obviously, companies have to pay attention to their product. They need to put time and effort into R&D and processes to make sure they create an excellent product. On the other hand, most businesses spend so much time on product that they don't have sufficient resources left over for thinking about the customer. This approach has never worked, and it certainly won't work in the future. Instead, you must continually consider what your customer really wants and innovate to provide it.

The funny thing is, when you open up more customer pathways, you start thinking about products in a whole new way. By keeping the customer first and foremost, you uncover fresh ideas for new products and open additional profit centers for existing products. You might find out that your customers wish you had a subscription service so they don't have to remember to buy your product every three months. Boom, you just opened up a new way of doing business that will benefit you greatly. It will lower your costs and improve revenue.

MYTH #4

You should use every avenue available to reach customers.

REALITY

You should prioritize the channels and tactics that will help you reach your goals.

Once you've researched your customer and know their journey, you'll start to have a clearer picture of which channels and tactics you should be focusing on. While you could try to do "all the things," most businesses don't have unlimited time or budget. If you create a comprehensive strategy that balances your short-term goals with long-term outcomes, you can narrow your focus to the most impactful channel mix.

THE CUSTOMER JOURNEY

Of course, just when you get to know someone, they go and change, right? Customers are no different. You're never talking to a static person; you're talking to someone who is on a journey. These days, that journey can include a lot of detours. Your job is to know where those detours are taking your customers. What patterns can you discern? Are they using a specific type of device? A specific channel? Is email influencing them, or is it billboards?

You're looking for touch points, predictable stages your customer goes through, with the goal of meeting them there. Meeting them where they are is a huge part of marketing success, and it's only going to be more so in the future.

Typically, customers go through the five broad stages listed below, but you can take away, add, and customize them in other ways to fit your specific customer journey:

1. **Awareness**—A person notices your brand or product. They may see an ad, a billboard, or read about you in an article. They may also become aware of a problem they have and start looking for a solution.

2. **Interest/Evaluation**—The customer is aware of a need they have and/or your brand. The potential customer starts to research their options. They may utilize search engines, ask friends, look at product comparison websites, or read reviews. They are looking to see if you are credible and will meet their needs.

3. **Action/Purchase**—They may become a customer at this point or they may have started a trial. Depending on the type of business, you might break these out into two different stages. One might be more focused on initial actions like downloading a resource, filling out a contact form, or joining your newsletter, and the other could be focused on when they have become a customer by making a purchase/commitment online or in person.

Unfortunately, many marketers think their job is done after they've completed a lead form or made a sale. I believe you should be looking at the complete customer journey, including their experience *after* the purchase.

If you do this, you will create a lot more loyal customers who will purchase from you again and sing your praises to others. This helps to fill your funnel with customers who already know you're a great and credible company.

4. **Experience**—You've got a new customer! Your job is not over, though. Actually, this is the most important part. What is your customer's experience with your service or product? As I mentioned before, customer experience will become a top-ranking factor. If you're not focusing on it, you're not likely to be in business ten years from now.

5. **Loyalty/Advocacy**—If they have a good experience, your customer may repeat a purchase and/or becomes a brand champion who starts marketing for you!

Let's look at a few of the questions or thoughts your customers might have at each stage:

AWARENESS

- Why is everybody talking about XYZ?
- What is this ad about? Have I seen that logo before?
- I'm too busy. I need someone to take over bookkeeping for my company so I can focus on growing it.

INTEREST/EVALUATION

- How would I benefit from this product/service in my life?
- How much does XYZ cost?
- What alternatives are out there?
- What do their reviews say? Are they reputable and stand behind their product?

ACTION/PURCHASE

- Do I have to give them my credit card to sign up for their free trial?
- Where can I buy XYZ?
- How much is shipping?
- Who has the best price? Who has the best product?
- How can I be certain of my satisfaction with this purchase?

EXPERIENCE

- Does this product or service meet my expectations?
- How do I reach customer support?
- How do I buy more?

LOYALTY/ADVOCACY

- I love this company/product/service. Who else could benefit from this?

- How can I use my reward points? Do they have any other products or services I could benefit from?
- How can I provide feedback to help them improve?

As you map out each stage for your customer, think about what they're feeling, thinking, and doing in each stage. What questions are they asking? You will want to have resources at the ready to answer their questions—and provide value—all throughout their journey.

You may uncover areas of the customer journey where your customers are feeling frustrated—thinking they may not be confident in making the decision to purchase or doing research where you don't even show up. These gaps are opportunities to improve the customer journey and experience and will ultimately help both of you reach your goals.

FUNNEL FOCUS

Many companies focus most of their efforts at the bottom of the funnel, in the action, or purchase stage. It's a good place to look, but they've come a little late to the party and missed out on the larger volume available in earlier stages. If you can capture the attention of people who are just curious, you can drive greater volumes of traffic to the action stage, too. By engaging with the customer early on, you're also developing a stronger relationship with them.

Wherever your customer is looking in each stage, whatever they're looking for, you need to show up and show up right away. I joked earlier about the death knell of landing on the second page of Google, but it's true—you don't want to be there.

To give you an example, we recently met with a well-known CBD oil (cannabis extract) company that was nowhere to be found in the first few pages of search. More than 800,000 people were searching for CBD oil-related terms each month, but the company had zero chance of engaging customers who were doing those searches. If you sell CBD oil, don't you think it would be valuable to show up when someone searches for "CBD oil"? Yes! Duh, right?

Since CBD oil was a newer product and hadn't passed the platform regulations of Google, Bing, Facebook, and Twitter, the company wasn't able to run paid ads. This meant that organic search represented the biggest opportunity for them, but they had yet to capitalize on it.

We met with their director of marketing, and I was excited to share this enormous opportunity with them. We shared a number of strategies that could help them get in front of the customers who were searching for their products. For example, they had a large list of retailers nationwide that sold their products, but the retailer directory on their website wasn't user or search engine friendly, and they could change that. We also shared that many of the searches for their products were local, which only expanded upon the opportunity. The director of marketing also had the idea of creating a downloadable CBD oil cookbook, and we thought that was a phenomenal idea. We explained the proper way to structure it to maximize visibility in search engines.

To make a long story short, rather than just creating a downloadable pdf, they could create a hub on their website with all of the different recipe categories so search engines could crawl and surface this information. Consumers could still download a pdf version, and they could also enter their email to be notified when new recipes were added. This could become a huge resource, bringing new and current customers to the site to find new recipes. The recipes would also be shareable so customers can tell their friends about it, bringing in even more customers.

If you understand the customer's journey, you can show up where they are looking, provide value, and create excitement. If, on the other hand, the customer shows up to your website and has a bad experience—maybe they have difficulty loading it, can't see it very well on their phone, or can't find the answer to their particular question—that's a check against you.

To meet customers where they are, you need to understand how they do things. The stages of the customer journey may be predictable, but as technology changes accelerate and devices and platforms proliferate, consumer behavior will continue to evolve. Many clients come to us with a strategy based on how they themselves behave online—they use certain keywords in certain search engines to find what they want, so they assume their customers will do the same.

The truth is, and this surprised me when I first discovered it over twelve years ago, everyone searches differently, especially now that we have voice search. When you analyze the keyword phrases people type in where your website comes up, you start to see that there are definitely some short-tail keywords with higher volume (one to two words in the search query), but you often see that the largest majority of your traffic comes from long-tail keywords (three-plus words). This realization led to a great habit of mine: I constantly question my own assumptions about people's habits, and instead, I research and find out what people are actually doing for each business or industry.

You won't necessarily discover the perfect pathway; customers won't always turn left at the end of the street where you expect them to. That's fine. What's important is that you understand what streets are frequently traveled so you can be visible to potential customers all along the journey.

TACTICS AND TOOLS

There are certain tactics and tools that can be utilized throughout all channels, and there are others that are channel specific. Search engine optimization (SEO) and search engine marketing (SEM) are specific to the search channel, but there is some overlap into the other channels, and the other channels can definitely benefit from these tactics if done correctly. Social media optimization (SMO) and paid social ads are of course utilized in the social channel. Email marketing, chatbots, text messaging, and push notifications are all categorized in the direct channel. All of these tactics can provide lift to the other channels.

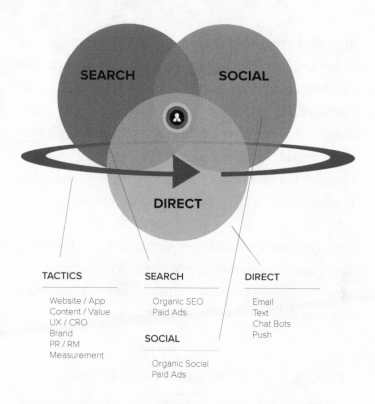

TACTICS	SEARCH	DIRECT
Website / App	Organic SEO	Email
Content / Value	Paid Ads	Text
UX / CRO		Chat Bots
Brand	**SOCIAL**	Push
PR / RM		
Measurement	Organic Social	
	Paid Ads	

The following strategies, tactics, and tools can (and should) be utilized throughout all channels to different extents depending on your specific strategy. Your brand and your messaging should be consistent across all channels, but your messaging may vary slightly depending on the specific audience.

Your website should be utilized to increase the effectiveness of all of these channels. Any useful and usable content should be repurposed and redistributed throughout these different channels. For example, you could spend hours working on a presentation and get value on only the one day you give the presentation, or you can record it and turn it into a video, podcast, webinar, multiple blog posts, and share it via social channels. You could compile it into a downloadable resource, include it in a book, upload your presentation to Slideshare or YouTube, optimize the content for search engines, and send it out to your audience via email or push notification.

Every channel can benefit from your public relations efforts (and vice versa), as well as help you with reputation management. Finally, all of these channels and tactics should be measured, which we'll discuss in more detail later.

GET A CLEAR PICTURE OF THE CUSTOMER

How do you get into your customer's mindset and tag along on their journey? In chapter 2, we introduced the concept of the customer persona, or archetype—a portrait of your customer. Here, we'll look at some of the ways you can create and use that portrait. The goal is to visualize your ideal customer or customers. Maybe it's stay-at-home fathers, or maybe it's single college students. Whatever it is, you might want to develop a few different archetypes to align with different products, or information, or whatever value you see yourself providing.

We did this with a medical clinic that had a very large

audience and served many communities. We had worked with them to develop a content strategy where each of their 250 physicians would create just one in-depth piece of content per year in their area of specialization. We knew this would be extremely valuable if it was done right, so we provided them with direction. We used some of their internal data from previous surveys as well as our own research to determine that they had five main audiences. We took these broad audiences and created five extremely detailed personas that included customer fears, uncertainties, desires, how they made decisions, and a number of other demographic and psychographic details. Now when they write their content, they can choose the most appropriate persona to write for.

If you're running a smaller business, you may not have the time or budget to spend a ton of time and money creating personas, but that doesn't mean you shouldn't do it. Personas don't have to be super-complex. Just by starting a persona, you put yourself in an empathetic state where you imagine yourself in your customers' shoes, and this is extremely valuable.

Personas can also be informative—if you know you're marketing to a thirty-year-old married woman with two kids who is looking to take a family vacation, you know a lot. Personas are only helpful, though, if you keep them top of mind throughout the marketing process. If you're going to put the time and resources into creating these customer portraits, make sure you use them. The good news is that creating personas will become easier over time, and in the future, you'll have no excuse not to. Analytics platforms, social platforms, and Integrated CRM (customer relationship management) data, for instance, are already making it much simpler to capture, collect, and then utilize that information at scale.

GETTING STARTED WITH STRATEGY

Identifying your ideal customer and understanding them better than anyone else is essential to developing a customer-centric digital marketing strategy. How well do you know your customers?

At Webfor, we try to find out more about our customers than just gender, age range, and title. Our job is to make them the hero in their business, so we need to know their challenges and fears. We want to know what keeps them up at night, what they desire, and what they're doing now that's misaligned with their goals. We want these people to succeed.

To develop your own customer-centric strategy, start by asking yourself some questions:

- Which customers do you love working with?
- Which customers does your team love to work with?
- Which customers can you provide the most value to?
- Which ones provide you with the most value?
- Who is the most loyal?
- Who could you get to endorse your product or service?
- Where can you interact with your customers?
- Where do your customers go to research your products? To buy your products?
- What is their buying process?
- What stages of the customer journey corresponds to the different channels?
- How will you engage your community?

Talk to some real customers and get real emotional responses. Customers might have been blown away by some small gesture you barely thought about; you can run with that and create more satisfied customers.

WHY DO YOU WANT TO ACHIEVE THIS GOAL?

I often say we would work with our customers for free if we could. We love them and what we do that much. As it is, we have to meet some business goals as well. As you dive deep into your customers' needs, don't forget your own bottom line; there's a reason you're doing all this inquiry. What are the major business objectives you want to accomplish?

COMMON OBJECTIVES:

- Increase revenue
- Improve profit
- Win/beat the competition
- Achieve your purpose: supporting the company's mission
- Increase market share
- Increase number of clients
- Retain clients
- Generate leads

QUESTIONS TO ASK YOURSELF:

- Why do people buy *your* product or service?
- What is the market valuation?
- How much revenue flows through different channels?

HOW WILL YOU GET THERE?

One of my favorite sayings is "What gets measured gets managed." This quote from Peter Drucker was in relation to management principles, but it also applies quite nicely to marketing. One of the things I love most about digital marketing is the ability to measure its effectiveness, and measuring your progress is the only way to know if you're reaching your goals. With that in mind, here are some more questions for you:

- What are the KPIs (key performance indicators) that will determine success?
- How will you track them?
- How will you budget to achieve them?
- Do you already have a budget? Is it realistic?
- When are you going to start?

FIVE MEANINGFUL METRICS

There are KPIs that every business should track to determine how well their marketing is working. What these metrics are and how often you look at them will vary greatly depending on your individual business, your customer, your industry, and your goals.

I recommended that you begin by defining what your goals are, because a goal is like a destination on a map. If you know where you're going and you know what the landmarks are along the way (your KPIs), then you can tell when you're getting closer to your goal or destination.

The following are five meaningful metrics that you should measure at minimum on a monthly basis.

UNIQUE VISITORS

You need to have optics on how many individual people are visiting your website. Are the number of potential customers coming to your website growing or decreasing? In order to understand the direction you're heading, you should also have month-over-month and year-over-year comparisons. While many businesses may have month-over-month downturns for a number of reasons (including seasonality), it's important to compare the same time period over the previous year.

Depending on your specific business needs, you can also create filtered views in Google Analytics to show only the most relevant stats. For instance, you can filter the view and remove visitors in other countries or other states, or you can filter out your blog traffic to see if traffic to your core pages is increasing.

CONVERSIONS

A conversion in digital marketing refers to a trackable action that you want the user to take on your website. This could be filling out a request for quote form, a contact form, downloading a resource, joining a newsletter, taking a quiz, viewing a coupon code, making a purchase, or even watching a video. If you can think of another action you want your customer to take, chances are you can track it as a conversion. For instance, if you want to track when a user gets directions to your store, views a key page on your website, or even uses the "click to call" feature on your mobile-optimized website, you can do that!

When we take a client over from another marketing agency, we find that most of the time they aren't tracking many of the important metrics. It's critical that you have these goals properly configured from the beginning so you can make decisions based on relevant, high-quality data. The good news: Google Analytics allows you to set up twenty of these different "goals" at no charge.

PHONE CALLS

Having a potential customer pick up the phone and call is the most desired action for many local businesses. They understand that this level of engagement converts at a much higher rate than the customer submitting a contact form and then moving on to research other vendors, yet the vast majority of businesses aren't tracking their calls.

When I say "tracking calls," I'm not just talking about the number of calls each week or month but tracking which media channels are generating these calls. If you're running ad campaigns, you'll want to know if they're producing phone calls, or if they're being driven by organic search. How many calls were driven by social media or that paid campaign? How can you optimize where you're investing your time and money if you aren't tracking this?

ENGAGEMENT

The definition of engagement will be different for each business. It's probably going to be a combination of metrics that give context as to how engaged your users are or how engaging the content on your website is. These can be metrics like time spent on your website, bounce rate, video play time, scroll depth, percentage of returning visitors, number of pages visited, and various other factors.

REVENUE

If you have an e-commerce store online, you can set up e-commerce tracking that allows you to pull in data from each sale. This allows you to see how much revenue is being generated by each marketing channel. You can determine which channels produce the highest number of sales, the average sale amount by channel, which products people purchased, as well as the devices people use to make these purchases. All of this can be tracked!

However, if your sales aren't made directly through your website, it can be much more challenging to tie revenue to specific metrics. In the marketing industry, this is referred to as the *attribution gap*. We've developed some pretty cool ways of being able to close this gap, but it often requires advanced integration with your Client Relationship Management (CRM) software or other manual workarounds.

TOOLS AND TIPS

Once you have identified an appropriate strategy for your business, you might look for help implementing it, or you might want to start putting it in motion on your own. If that's you, here are a few tools and tips I've found especially helpful (please see the appendix for a more comprehensive list).

GOOGLE ANALYTICS

Google Analytics will provide data on visitors who are visiting your website and give you more detail about your customer. It not only tracks and reports website traffic but can also help you gather more specific demographic and psychographic information. You can find out more about what market segment your website visitors are in, what other pages they like to visit, average ages, gender, and even some of their interests.

FACEBOOK TRACKING PIXEL

You can install the Facebook tracking pixel on your website, create a custom audience, and access a veritable fire hose of data. When people visit your website and have a Facebook account (which would be most people), they will be added (it's all anonymous of course) to the custom audience you created. You can view this custom audience to see some of the top pages your visitors like, their age and gender breakdowns, job titles, relationship statuses, and their education level.

GATHERUP

GatherUp is a great tool to create a customer feedback loop, measure your customer experience, and drive more online reviews. It contains a rich feature set for tracking your overall net promoter score (NPS), and with customer experience increasing in importance, you'll want to see how the changes you make improve customer satisfaction.

SURVEYMONKEY

Surveys are great tools you can use to reach out to your customers, once you've built a customer list. Services like SurveyMonkey make it easy for you and the survey recipient. To encourage participation, be sure to let survey-takers know that your goal is not to sell them something but to understand them better and improve your level of service. You might also offer an incentive—a gift card giveaway for the first five responders, for instance. They also have a free option that works for many businesses.

CRYSTALKNOWS

One of my favorite data-gathering tools is a service

called CrystalKnows, which allows you to apply a popular behavioral assessment tool—the DISC profile—using publicly available information, such as a LinkedIn profile. The DISC analysis describes your customer based on four personality traits:

- **D—Dominance.** The D style tends to be direct, firm, or even forceful. They value taking action, getting results, and are generally competitive.
- **I—Influence.** The I style tends to be outgoing, enthusiastic, and are generally optimistic in nature. Like the D style, they like to take action but are more collaborative than competitive.
- **S—Steadiness.** The S style tends to be patient and accommodating. They enjoy stability, and much like the I style, they tend to be collaborative and enjoy being helpful.
- **C—Conscientiousness.** The C style is usually analytical and reserved. Similar to the S style, they prefer stability, but they value accuracy, which causes them to challenge assumptions.

We've had the opportunity to apply the DISC profile in many situations. For example, we've discovered that business owners tend to be more high-D individuals who make decisions quickly and focus on outcomes, so when we talk to them, we help them keep their eyes on the prize, because that's what they value. We also understand that they can sometimes come across as abrasive, but they also like it when you're blunt with them so we can communicate very directly to them. Your customer, on the other hand, might score higher on conscientiousness, and if you know that, you can emphasize accuracy, expertise, and competency in your messaging.

It's important to note that everyone is a combination of these four personality traits; people are dynamic, and they aren't limited to just one.

CLARITAS

These days, you can discover an amazing amount of information about who your customers are. Claritas has taken the entire US population and broken it down into sixty-eight different segments. These "segments" are basically personas that provide demographic and psychographic data. You can browse the different segments and see the areas where that segment lives, their income, their job title, the kind of car they drive, and even the kinds of restaurants they frequent. If you find a segment that is a clear match for your customer, this is great to use for inspiration.

UXPRESSIA

With this tool, you can visualize, analyze, export, and

share customer journeys and personas. You can use it to add the customer's picture and some background information, everything from what frustrations they might have, to things you should never do. Also good to know.

We've covered a lot in these last couple of chapters. We discussed how to uncover what your customers are doing and how to really understand them. We discussed the customer journey, and I shared a few of the tools and tactics you can use to help gain this understanding. We talked about some of the key elements to developing a customer-centric marketing strategy and using competitive intelligence to gain insights into additional opportunities. That's a lot!

Once you are up to speed and get a really good understanding of your customer and their journey, and you develop a strategy based on those insights, you'll want to start anticipating their next move so you can be one step ahead.

PART II

NAVIGATING A NEW MARKETING LANDSCAPE

CHAPTER FIVE

WHERE THEY'RE GOING NEXT

WHAT'S CHANGING IN YOUR CUSTOMERS' WORLD

In part 1, we explored the current marketing landscape, learned how to find out who our customers are, what they're doing, and how to develop a strategy to get the right message in front of them at the right time. I realize all of that fills up your plate and then some, but please don't leave the table just yet, because there's a whole new menu coming out. People are not only accessing your search, social, and direct channels—they're beginning to use digital assistants that rely on artificial intelligence (AI) to gain entry to those channels. Some people are embracing this shift, while others are moving cautiously, and that's no surprise. It's what humans have always done with big technological advances, at least since the Industrial Revolution.

THE MORE THINGS CHANGE

It's difficult to imagine now, but before the Industrial Revolution, everything was powered by either a human or an animal. Humans owned power, so when the steam engine came along, it seemed threatening; many people protested the change. The same thing happened when factories started producing goods that had once been made by hand. People worried about being replaced by machinery.

While the Industrial Revolution certainly changed the way people work, it didn't replace them—they found new ways to work in the new economy. Still, people continued to be wary of new technology, often to a degree that seems ludicrous to us now. When the telephone first became popular, there were rumors that the dead could talk to you through the phone line. Some people thought cameras could capture your soul. When people panicked over the PC revolution, we even coined a phrase for it: "computer phobia." It wasn't long, though, before people used computers for everything—including accessing a nifty new invention called the internet. Then mobile phones were introduced, and people began using those more frequently than computers.

The disruption never stops, because we're always looking for ways to grow and improve. Few people today worry about ghosts in the phone lines, and in the age of the selfie, we certainly don't seem concerned about the camera stealing our soul. Some people may still suffer from computer phobia, but for the most part, we look back at these shifts and realize the benefits we've received—from increased production and sales from manufacturing to the ability to communicate instantly with people all over the world.

Still, we're a little less sanguine when we hear the words "artificial intelligence." That's understandable. Up until now, humans have owned intelligence. Of course, we wonder if artificial intelligence will displace us, like we once feared steam-powered engines and manufacturing robots. And we've all seen *Terminator*, right?

I have no doubt we will come to appreciate the opportunities inherent in the new technology as we always have, but this shift is different because it's going to happen much, much faster. The Industrial Revolution took its time, unfolding over several decades, but with the exponential pace of technology development today, society won't have nearly as much time to adjust.

We can get a good start, however, by considering the intelligent tools we're already using and a few cutting-edge innovations that are on the horizon.

SMARTER THAN YOU THINK

Have you ever tried to learn the game of "Go"? It's a deceptively simple-looking board game where two players place black and white stones on a crosshatched wooden board. Go masters spend many years playing and are never able to exhaust all of the possible moves. Google's computer program, AlphaGo, on the other hand, was able to beat a professional Go player in 2015. By 2016, a subsequent version of the program beat the number-one-ranked Go player in the world, eighteen-time world champion Lee Sedol.

AlphaGo doesn't represent the kind of artificial intelligence most people think of when they think "AI." Most AI like AlphaGo is *vertical AI,* meaning that it is good at a specific task like playing a game or image recognition. However, what most people envision when they think of AI is referred to as AGI, or *artificial general intelligence.* This type of AI doesn't yet exist and would have the ability to do many different skills, perform multiple tasks, understand language, recognize images, and even communicate. There are many predictions of when we'll see AGI, but most experts are saying in the next ten to fifty years.

One thing's for sure, someday we'll look back on the processing speed of today, which once seemed so impressive, and just laugh. The AI of the future will work on a much higher level. It will understand language, process images, and predict trends faster than ever before.

SEMANTIC SEARCH

The new AI owes much to visionaries like Ray Kurzweil, genius, futurist, author, and founder of multiple companies. Kurzweil, who had never worked for anyone else in his life, inexplicably went to work for Google in 2013. Their projects were interesting but relatively mundane. He was in charge of Talk to Books—a search engine for books that was able to read and understand text at an unfathomable speed. He was also involved in revamping and rolling out Google's Smart Reply feature, which uses contextual clues to finish your sentences when you're writing an email.

Many people are still scratching their heads. Why is a genius like Ray Kurzweil so involved in these seemingly mundane efforts? If you understand where they're going, then it's easier to connect the dots. Their goal is not just to build the best search engine but ultimately to develop an intelligent digital assistant—a companion that would understand and be able to communicate effectively with people. That companion would have to learn from huge data sets, things like the content of all the world's books and the billions of email conversations being sent every day. It also needed to understand concepts and intent, not just identify keywords. Kurzweil was essentially building the training wheels for "semantic search," which allows a computer program, or an algorithm, to learn the meaning behind language and understand how conversations work. Semantic search is one of the foundational elements for the intelligent digital assistant.

Natural language processing (NLP), the ability for computers to understand language, has grown at an exponential rate in the last five years. Just think about how much better voice search has become over that time. With the development of artificial intelligence and deep neural networks that are modeled after our own brain, these computer programs can utilize something called word vectors to understand the relationship between words. Language is very hierarchical and these vector models allow the intelligent program to learn, remember, and recognize these language patterns. This is the reason Gmail can understand the email you received, develop an intelligent response, and finish your sentences as well.

Did you know that 15 percent of the searches performed on Google are brand new to them? Could you imagine how big of a problem this would be for a search engine that is trying to provide the best results for its users? In 2015, Google announced RankBrain, a machine learning algorithm that uses an interpretation model to determine the intent behind a user's query and provide the most relevant search results. Initially, it was just being used to process the 15 percent of searches that were brand new, but by 2016, machine learning was being applied to all queries.

What does this mean? It means that the importance no longer lies in just the keywords used in a search query or on a web document—it's the user's intent behind the words that holds more weight. Does your content provide tremendous value to satisfy the intent of the user's query? In addition, search engines are using similar technology to understand entities, people, places, and things, as well as their relationship to each other. They understand not just "strings" of words but also things in context.

Can I use you as a guinea pig for a second? Just play along with me. Assuming you have a smartphone and know how to use voice search, pull out your phone and perform the following voice searches on Google.

Prompt voice search and say, "How tall is the Statue of Liberty?" Google should reply with something along the lines of, "The Statue of Liberty is 305 feet tall."

Now perform another voice search and say, "Where is it?" Google will reply with, "The Statue of Liberty is located in New York."

That second question didn't have your keywords in it, but based on your search session history, Google determined that when you said "it," you're referring to the Statue of Liberty. This is just one small example of how search engines are better understanding their customers and providing a better customer experience. Search engines know that they need to provide high-quality experiences or else their users will go elsewhere.

One such collection of elements they look at is called EAT. This acronym stands for expertise, authority, and trust. Google utilizes this term heavily throughout their own search quality evaluator guidelines. Search engines of course look at your content to determine EAT, but in addition, they're also looking at the source of that content. Is the author an expert in that topic? Are they a trusted and authoritative source? Do they work for a brand that is considered authoritative in the larger category?

Many of these topics I discussed above are the first layer of the brain of the intelligent digital assistant that many companies are trying to build. If you want to position yourself for success in the future, you can start delivering in these areas now.

QUANTUM COMPUTING

This futuristic digital assistant would be impossible to

pull off without adequate computing power to process all of the data that's being gathered. As usual, Ray Kurzweil was way ahead of us on this. If you were impressed by the prescience of Moore's law, coined in 1965 by Intel founder Gordon Moore—the observation that the number of processors on a computer chip doubled every year while the cost halved—hold onto your hat, because here comes the law of accelerating returns:

> *"Fundamental measures of information technology follow predictable and exponential trajectories."*

That exponential trajectory means we don't just double processing power every year; we also compound it with every investment we make in digital technology. Kurzweil often illustrates his theory with the story of a chess game in which the player places a single grain of rice on the first square, two on the second, four on the third, and so on. The first turns of the game are fairly unimpressive, but the doublings soon wind up requiring a chessboard bigger than twice the surface of the earth.

Quantum computing could make this incredible leap possible. Theoretically, a quantum computer could be more powerful than the most powerful supercomputers used today.

Currently, the online experience is affected by limited

processing power. Depending on the type of connection a user has, it could take anywhere from a minute to five minutes to download a movie. While that's a huge improvement over just a few years ago when an hour-long video could take all day to download, it's going to get much faster.

In the future, thanks to quantum computing and other advancements in technology, user experience will be greatly improved. It will also look different. When we overcome speed limitations, we gain the ability to gather even more data and provide an even richer experience. Much of that data will likely be visual, as AI begins to understand video, audio, and images better. AI has already made significant leaps in the area of computer vision and, in many cases, can understand an image better than a human. In the future, people will be able to pinpoint a conversation between movie characters simply by asking their assistant about it, even if they can't recall any of the actual words.

FUTURE IMPACT

Artificial intelligence and quantum computing will make all sorts of exciting things happen—from self-driving cars to smart medical devices—but they will also have a practical impact on the day-to-day world of everyday businesspeople.

Currently, there a number of tools available to translate your website into other languages, but they aren't search engine friendly, and they don't translate the content as well as a human translator. That's going to change. One of the things we're excited about at Webfor is simplifying the process to create multiple versions of a website that target different countries and in different languages. We can do that today, but it's a complex process. To create the sites, we have to use a translator to translate all of the content, create additional pages (or an entirely different website), and mark up the content in specific ways so search engines will recognize which language the site uses and what country it is targeting.

We also have to mark up the content using what's called an *hreflang tag* to make sure that search engines understand that a website with similar content in English for the United Kingdom is indeed targeting the UK; we don't want them to treat it as duplicate content and ignore it. As natural language processing improves along with technology, we'll be able to translate a website into multiple different languages at the click of a button.

Advances in artificial intelligence and just technology in general are going to provide a tremendous number of opportunities to improve efficiency and effectiveness. Forward-thinking businesses are already leveraging a number of these to give themselves a competitive advantage. Speaking of a competitive advantage, one huge competitive advantage you can have is knowing by understanding how the landscape is changing. In the next chapter, I will share the trends that are shaping the future of marketing.

CHAPTER SIX

THE THREE Ps

PERSONALIZED, PREDICTIVE, AND PROACTIVE

As important as it is now to be in the right place at the right time to meet your particular customer at various turning points in their journey, it's only going to become more crucial as technological changes accelerate.

It can be daunting to think about just how much is going to change. When I started thinking about this back in 2015, I realized it would be impossible for us to process each of the millions of changes coming our way, so I began trying to identify the larger patterns. As I looked for macro trends that would be consistent over a long period, I recognized that marketing would continue to change in three ways:

It would become more Personalized, more Predictive, and more Proactive.

Personalization was perhaps the most obvious theme, given advancements in technology and the younger generation's expectation and demand that their online experience be tailored to their preferences. At the same time, more powerful, cheaper computing power was making it possible to process massive amounts of data—data that would allow us to better predict outcomes. Advances such as semantic search promised the ability to understand user intent to the extent that we could capture the holy grail of marketing—we could proactively offer our customers the personalized service they wanted before they even knew they wanted it.

Right now, customers aren't customers until they recognize a need and ask a question. To some extent, you can wait for them to come to you. If someone spills ketchup on their shirt at lunch, for example, they may realize they need a dry cleaner and ask their digital assistant to find one.

In the not-too-distant future, the person's digital assistant might notice the stain and offer the phone number of a convenient dry cleaner open during hours that match the person's schedule, along with the address of a nearby store that carries the same size and style of shirt. If you're a dry cleaner or a men's clothing store, you need that digital assistant to know about you and recommend you.

This shift—from reactive to proactive—represents a fundamental change in the way people and technology interact. It's such a major shift that some people may initially protest; perhaps they're not sure they want a digital assistant to know that much about them. I believe we will get acclimated, though. People already value some fairly proactive technology—when their phone reports an accident on their usual route to work and recommends leaving twenty minutes earlier, they are pleasantly surprised. Very soon, they'll be ready to enter a world where every digital assistant provides a personalized, predictive, and proactive experience to the user.

GETTING TO KNOW YOU: PERSONALIZED INTERACTIONS

Have you ever received an email newsletter that's not personalized to you in any way? Did you read it? Probably not—non-personalized messages fail at a high rate. When I began thinking about the Three Ps, I realized my interactions with digital assistants were similarly anonymous. I was constantly frustrated by their inability to know when it was me on the other end of the conversation. Whether the assistant was on a phone, computer, or other device, it couldn't tell the difference between me asking a question and my son asking a question. It was a little like getting a generic email—I wasn't compelled to engage.

Today, through preference setups and voice training, your assistant knows that it's talking to you. You can ask your assistant to add items to your grocery list, schedule meetings on your calendar, or tell it to turn off the lights in your bedroom at night and wake you up in the morning with your favorite song. I love using Google Maps, for example, because I can specify the types of restaurants I like and don't like, so I get results tailored to my needs.

In the future, this setup will be even easier to perform; it's likely to unfold like a real conversation. Like any good assistant, human or machine, your assistant is going to ask lots of questions to get to know you, and you'll be most responsive if it asks those questions in a comfortable, conversational style: "Are there specific restaurants you love? Do you want me to add those to your list? Are there certain types of food you like? Are there certain types of food you don't like or are allergic to?" All you have to do is speak your answer.

People are generally comfortable with this type of personalization, because they choose to provide the information and make the requests. If I didn't want an assistant to know about me, I simply wouldn't enter any information.

The assistant of the future will take personalization a step further. It will integrate your answers with what it knows about you from other sources, like your conversation history. Take the following interaction as an example:

You have been planning a trip to London. You're having coffee with a friend and talking about all the locations you want to visit. Suddenly, you remember that you need to renew your passport and get a new suitcase. You mention this to your friend, and because your assistant is in "listen mode," it automatically determines that these are important follow-up items.

After you finish your coffee and conclude the conversation with your friend, your assistant sends a notification to your phone. The notification reads, "IMPORTANT: To be able to travel to London in June, you need to file passport renewal paperwork no later than next week and choose expedited service. Here is the link, with your information prefilled. Please select your preferred passport photo, gather the required identification documents, and select how you'd like to pay.

Shortly after, you get another notification: The places you want to visit in London sound very nice. Would you like me to add them to your "Want to Go" list?

Later that afternoon, you get another prompt. It says, "I've done some research on the top places to visit while in London, the best places to stay, and have also found a few differ-

ent luggage options since you mentioned you needed a new suitcase. It appears that you're driving. Would you like to review this in conversation mode via text prompts, or not at all?" You say, *"Conversation mode,"* and your assistant begins by greeting you and saying, *"Good afternoon, Jennifer. I hope you're having a good day. I've found three suitcases that I believe would be suitable based on your past purchase history. Would you like to review the features, benefits, and pricing of each one individually? Or would you like for me to send you the one I think best fits your needs?"* You respond by saying, *"Send me the one that you think is best for my needs."*

Your assistant continues, *"I've noticed you haven't booked your flight or hotel yet for London. Would you like for me to monitor prices and find the best options?"* You say, *"Yes, please,"* because you want to be polite, even to a computer. It asks you a few more questions on your flight and hotel preferences and whether your husband and kids will be traveling with you. Then it starts to research the best options and pricing, and it predicts the best time to purchase.

"One last thing, Mrs. Jennifer, based on your previous travels, you seem to like visiting places that have nice views and lively bar scenes. There is a popular travel destination called the Shard that has a restaurant on the thirty-first floor with views of London. It also has a number of items on the menu you might like. Would you like to learn more?"

This may sound very futuristic, but it isn't as far off as you might think. We're not quite to the point where digital assistants know exactly what each individual is looking for, but they are using predictive analytics and machine learning to better understand how to provide the most satisfying results. They can categorize audiences by intent, place them in market segments, and show them information that's likely to resonate.

Ultimately, personalized digital assistants will probably restore a lot of our personal time, because we won't be as frantic and busy taking care of details. They will actually allow us to be more present with the people in our lives. It's going to be a dramatic change at a societal level, on par with or surpassing the Industrial Revolution, but I imagine we will look back and wonder how we ever lived without our personalized digital assistants.

When that shift happens, it will offer a huge opportunity for businesses. As we've seen, understanding the customer is key to success in marketing, and we're about to understand them better than ever before. Right now, we're marketing to an audience, not a person; digital marketing today is a bit like walking into a convention and approaching each person there with the same speech. We'll reach some people that way because we know, generally, who is in the room, but we'll also alienate others. The more we can tailor our communications, the closer we get to having meaningful, one-to-one conversations with individual customers.

With personalization, we're looking the customer in the eye, learning about their individual needs, and adjusting our message on the fly to help them understand how we can help them. This is not optional, because people are going to expect it even more in the future.

ONE STEP AHEAD: PREDICTIVE TECHNOLOGIES

As important as it is to know who your customer is and what they're doing, how great would it be to know what they're going to do next? Soon we will. We all have predictable patterns of behavior, after all, whether we recognize it or not. You probably get up at a similar time each day, eat the same type of breakfast, pour the same brand of coffee, and drive the same roads to work. Predictive technology can observe all of that and warn you before you run out of coffee or suggest you leave ten minutes early because an accident is backing up traffic on your preferred route. Once you're at work, your assistant could recognize that you're overloaded with emails and respond to some on your behalf.

And you won't have to ask for any of this help. Predictive assistants won't require you to make a query. For example, my wife and I go on a date night every week. Right now, I might ask my assistant to recommend a restaurant or a movie. In the future, my assistant will predict that I'll want ideas for date night and offer them up. It might say something like, "You guys always go down to Urban Farmers restaurant for dinner on your date night. I can make your reservations and send you an email reminder if you like."

Most people are going to love having an assistant that appears to read their mind. (An assistant that helps me respond to high-priority emails *and* makes sure I never forget my wife's birthday again? I'm in!) Others will be more cautious, wondering if they are controlling the predictive technology or the technology is controlling them.

Similarly, most companies are going to embrace predictive technology, because being one step ahead of the customer is an enormous advantage. If you can predict their needs, deliver on them, and provide more value than anyone else, you will create amazing experiences for your customers. You'll also get more customers, because there's no better marketing than a satisfied customer. You'll gain endorsers and brand champions who will spread the word about their experience and transfer their enthusiasm to new customers.

The ability to predict which people are going to have a higher propensity to buy your product or service also gives you a huge benefit, because it allows you to focus more on the people who are really interested in what you're doing. For example, Salesforce uses machine learning, a subset of artificial intelligence, to predict which leads will convert at a higher rate. They don't just count traffic; they gather data over time to show who becomes a customer and how. Analyzing that data can reveal customer patterns, like the fact that 40 percent of visitors convert after visiting three specific pages, or that 60 percent of leads that download a specific resource become a customer. You might discover that if they do all of these things, there's a 70 percent chance they'll become a customer. You can use that information to allocate your resources wisely—you probably want to send your best salespeople after the high-probability customers and place less emphasis on one-time web visitors.

Again, we're not there yet. On a scale of 1 to 10, we're probably at a 3 in terms of where we will be in the next ten years. In specific instances, however, we're quite good at predicting consumer behavior. We can predict traffic patterns pretty accurately, for instance, to determine that a certain percentage of people will take route A and another percentage will take route B. We can analyze how people come into a store and how they shop as well, but we can't generalize.

Different platforms have different strengths here. Google,

for instance, can tell by search behavior which people can effectively be targeted with car ads, but it doesn't understand who your friends are. Google knows what you're searching for, but Facebook knows your likes, dislikes, education, job title, friend network, and so on. Fortunately for marketers, they don't keep that information to themselves; you can generate a tailored customer list—a lookalike audience—based on a current customer's data. You can get a lot of value out of that, though you won't be able to pinpoint an individual's needs just yet. That day will come, however, and we want to be ready for it, so we have to start thinking about what consumers are going to want and how they're going to behave in the future. As Google said in their twenty-year anniversary blog post, it's time for businesses to start predicting consumers' needs.[4]

MAY I SUGGEST PROACTIVE ASSISTANCE

People will be pretty happy with assistants that offer personal, predictive service, but that's not all they want. Think about it—if you were going to hire a personal assistant, what would your expectations be? Yes, you would want them to be personalized, to know you and understand your needs, but you would also want them to

---

4   Ken Wheaton, "20 years in, search has become a powerful personal assistant," thinkwithgoogle.com, September 2018, https://www.thinkwithgoogle.com/advertising-channels/search/search-strategy/.

predict, to some degree, how you go about fulfilling your needs. That's great, but how frustrated would you feel if your assistant didn't follow through and just waited for your request? If you have to ask your assistant to order a coffee every morning or to check your schedule weekly to identify conflicts, you might save yourself a little time, but you might also get pretty frustrated. You would probably much rather have an assistant that's independent and proactive—taking care of you by staying one step ahead and offering solutions to problems you may not have even recognized yet.

The proactive assistant orders your coffee so it's ready for you every weekday at 7:30 a.m. It sees that you have some mismatches in your schedule and suggests changes to make it work better. When that happens, pretty much everybody is going to want in.

The dawn of the truly proactive assistant will mark a fundamental change in digital marketing. We will go from a situation where we wait for a prompt from the customer before we can offer up solutions, to a world where we can surface content the potential customer hadn't even considered yet. Right now, a search for flight schools would bring up just that—a list of flight schools. The searcher might see a few ads along the way, and those ads might drive traffic and revenue, which is useful but limited. A proactive assistant would know that you've set a goal of learning to fly in ten years and offer up a variety of resources. Now you see not just flight school ads but also an amateur pilots' forum and articles about learning to fly. What's more, the assistant doesn't forget but reminds you, "Hey, you set a goal of ten years to learn to fly. They will politely prompt you down the funnel. Did you know that it takes an average of two to three years to get through flight school? Would you like me to make an inquiry?"

The blog written by Google, "Improving Search for the Next 20 Years," supports these macro trends in a recent post:

> As Google marks our 20th anniversary, I wanted to share a first look at the next chapter of Search, and how we're working to make information more accessible and useful for people everywhere. This next chapter is driven by three fundamental shifts in how we think about Search:
>
> The shift from answers to journeys: To help you resume tasks where you left off and learn new interests and hobbies, we're bringing new features to Search that help you with ongoing information needs.
>
> The shift from queries to providing a queryless way to get to information: We can surface relevant information related to your interests, even when you don't have a specific query in mind.

And the shift from text to a more visual way of finding infor-
mation: We're bringing more visual content to Search and
completely redesigning Google Images to help you find infor-
mation more easily.[5]

To be that proactive, assistants will most likely have a "listen mode" to gather information from the things you talk about. This mode will allow them to proactively determine and provide useful information or actions. If you were talking to a colleague about having lunch next Tuesday, your assistant could pop up and ask, "Hey, would you like me to schedule that appointment in your calendar?" All you have to do is say yes.

That "listening" type of behavior can be very efficient. Imagine an assistant that takes notes in a meeting, highlights action items, and issues a schedule of assignments. That would save a lot of time. Still, the idea of a machine that listens concerns some people. It's helpful to explain that today's assistants, such as Cortana, Alexa, or Siri, are not eavesdropping on conversations. They're listening for a keyword and only activate when that word is spoken. In the future, I imagine we will come to a point where the digital assistant is always on, or where there are different versions, paid and unpaid, with different levels of service. People will still be able to turn it off.

---

5   Ben Gomes, "Improving Search for the next 20 years," blog.google, September 24, 2018, https://www.blog.google/products/search/improving-search-next-20-years/.

Because of privacy concerns, proactive tech may be a hard sell at first, but I believe people will come to value it. Google Discover is already demonstrating that. It knows what I want to know more about; I don't have to go out and search for it, because it shows up in my Discover feed. I love it, and apparently others see the value, too—800 million people are already using it.[6] Google recently added the ability to see stats in Google Search Console to show how a website was benefiting from the Discover feed. At the time of this writing, one of our clients received 100K impressions and over 7,000 clicks to their website in the last thirty days just from this feature alone!

Most businesses are still largely reactive, not because seeing this future requires a crystal ball, but simply because they are scrambling to focus on "the now." They're not unaware of the direction digital marketing is taking, they're just so engrossed in their current business that they don't take time to strategize, plan for the future, and anticipate the customer's needs. Companies that do manage to focus on the future, or engage partners who can help them do that, stand a much better chance of taking advantage of the change as it unfolds. Businesses like Amazon get this—they want people to be prompted to buy products that are sold on their site. With proac-

---

6   Karen Corby, "Discover new information and inspiration with Search, no query required," blog. google, https://www.blog.google/products/search/introducing-google-discover/.

tive marketing that's always on, they don't have to wait for customers to decide to look for something, go to the phone, type in or voice a query, and place an order.

COMBINING THE THREE PS

Moving from reactive to proactive technology will offer huge benefits to users and the companies that serve them. That's why we, as marketers, need to understand how to provide value to the customer in the new environment.

As you grow in your ability to deliver service that embodies all of the Three Ps, that personalized, predictive, and proactive approach will open up a world of opportunities. It will allow you to create excellent experiences for your customers and build a robust reputation for your company and brand. Regardless of what stage of the journey people are in, those who enjoy working with you will start to think of you as a good company in general and recommend you to their friends. Ultimately, that means more customers in your funnel.

Beyond the bottom line, I think marketers are going to find working in the new paradigm very satisfying. I know I find joy in being able to really make a difference in the life of a customer. If you're passionate about serving your customer, delivering more value than ever, and doing it more effectively and efficiently than ever before, then the world is about to be your oyster!

CHAPTER SEVEN

THE NEW DIGITAL ASSISTANT

HOW WILL IT HELP YOU?

The notification came at 11:32 a.m.

"Hey, there's a place on your 'want to go' list right around the corner."

I hadn't thought about this place in a while, but it was almost lunchtime, and I did want to try it, so I turned left where I would have otherwise turned right. And a new restaurant customer was born!

That's just one example of the power of a personalized, predictive, and proactive digital assistant. It may sound futuristic, but it's already in action. Take these familiar features, for example:

- A notification pops up on your phone, reminding you when your next appointment is.
- Another one pops up letting you know that you'll need to leave in ten minutes if you want to get to your next appointment on time, because there's heavy traffic on your route.
- Your smartwatch reminds you it's time to take a break or a breath.
- A search engine replies to your voice search for "Hotels in Kissimmee, Florida" with the results and a voice response asking you if you know which dates you're traveling. Then after you reply, it asks if you'd like to narrow the results by star rating, budget, or amenities.
- Your car "sees" the vehicle in front of you, slows down, and applies the brake.

That's only the beginning, of course. The assistants of the future will be much more advanced. We may see robots that can understand emotions based on facial expression and tone of voice. By reading biometrics, an assistant could detect a medical emergency and dial 911; by listening, it could detect frustration and turn on some soothing music.

Overall, this technology will be more integrated into

everyday life. It's already working in sync with household products such as light bulbs and refrigerators. Assistants will soon be able to help people determine optimum nutrition and even alert them when they're becoming dehydrated. This type of technology is only going to become increasingly ubiquitous.

RISING TO THE CHALLENGES

Some people will celebrate all of these innovations right away, while others will express concerns. They may feel like their privacy is being invaded or worry that the assistant is always listening or watching them. The anxiety mounts as they think about who might use their information once it's out of their control. I get it; I've had some of the same concerns myself. What I've discovered, though, is that the more I understand about the technology, the more comfortable I get. Plus, understanding puts the power back in our hands—if we understand it, we can shape it to work the way we want it to.

As the technology matures, we're putting more controls in place. You probably remember the stream of privacy notifications that flooded your email in May 2018, thanks to the General Data Protection Regulation (GDPR) passed by the European Union. GDPR sets requirements for the way companies handle personal data and how they disclose data collection, which resulted from people's number one fear about new technology: the invasion of privacy. It's little wonder people are concerned; more data is being collected about them than ever before. Remember, our ability to collect and parse massive amounts of data is what makes smart digital assistants possible, and that data has to come from somewhere.

It's interesting to note, however, that as a society we are adjusting to the notion that our personal information is widely available. Baby boomers seem to be more reluctant to share with the masses, but millennials appear to be more comfortable with it. When you're using technology to reach customers, it's important to respect their level of comfort. The best way to do that is by using the technology to provide value while maintaining a human touch. It's a delicate balancing act.

Going back to chatbots as an example, they offer tremendous opportunity to interact with people on their customer journey. Chatbots can reach out on your behalf and initiate conversations with prospective customers. You can set a bot to notice when someone comments on a Facebook message and then approach the commenter via Facebook Messenger. "Hey, thanks for your comment," it might say. "I'd love to know more. Are you a business owner, a marketer, or an executive?" If they answer, the bot can continue to engage them, sending out new messages over time.

Similarly, you can use a tracking pixel on your website to build a list of people who have visited your website. That's an incredible opportunity for remarketing—now you're able to show them your ads while they're browsing the web or checking out social media and encourage them to come back to your site. People understand that you're going to do that to some extent, but if an ad with the same pair of boots follows them around for thirty days straight, they're not going to form a warm, fuzzy feeling about you. They may feel more like they're being stalked. You're better off setting a frequency cap that limits how often they'll see impressions from your ads and for how long.

In the future, the assistant will make a lot of assumptions based on what it knows about you from a variety of sources, not from what you choose to tell it. If you're looking for a new restaurant to take your spouse to, it will draw on what it knows about the places you've gone before, reviews you've written, and conversations you've had. It will probably even know that your spouse prefers a restaurant with gluten-free options.

The methods mentioned above offer opportunities for marketers because they drive customers further down the sales funnel. In a way, the assistant is the one going through the customer journey now. If you want to be the restaurant that lands at the top of the assistant's list of recommendations, you need to understand how the algorithm makes decisions so you can optimize your content to be discovered by them. Just make sure you're still optimizing for the *person* and not just the algorithm, because there's a fine line between being proactive and being pushy.

PROMISE ON THE HORIZON

Like every other technological shift since the Industrial Revolution, it will take a while for society to adjust to the presence of increasingly personalized, predictive, and proactive technology in their lives. However, I think people will embrace it fairly quickly once they understand how valuable these new smart assistants will be in their everyday lives. Here are a few promising innovations already rolling out:

CONVERSATIONAL ASSISTANTS

One of the most exciting innovations in digital-assistant technology is their ability to hold a natural-feeling conversation. Just last year, Google launched "Continued Conversation" for Google Assistant, which allowed for follow-up questions and interactions without having to say, "OK, Google" every time. Shortly after, Amazon launched something they called "Follow-Up Mode." While these are huge advancements, they still don't have the feeling of a real conversation with a human.

Voice search is all the rage right now, but it is just the beginning. As technology matures, we'll move from voice search to conversational search. Strangely, at that point we'll be asking ourselves if we still call it "search." Maybe we'll just refer to it as "assistance."

This ability to hold a natural-feeling conversation took a major leap when Google unveiled its new technology, Duplex, in 2018. Google Duplex is an artificially intelligent chat agent that sounds almost indistinguishable from a real person. Duplex uses natural language processing to both understand and generate language to carry on a conversation.

That year at Google I/O, they said it is their vision to have their assistant help you get things done and that a large part of that is making phone calls or having conversations. To demonstrate, they requested that the assistant call to schedule a hair appointment at a salon. It sounds almost indistinguishable from a real person, and its ability to understand even broken English was impressive. It even uses natural human language tendencies, like saying "Mm-hmmm" when we mean "yes." It also pauses in a reassuringly human way and waits for you to reply. If you haven't seen or heard Google Duplex in action, you should look at this video right now.

https://youtu.be/-qCanuYrRog

This feature started rolling out on Google's Pixel phone at the end of 2018, and near the end of Q1, it rolled out to other smartphones, including iPhones. Currently, Duplex is mainly used to make reservations or book a haircut so you don't have to do that yourself, but in the not-so-distant future, I see the ability to schedule your appointments, answer your phone calls (this is already happening on Pixel phones), or arrange meetings with multiple parties. Busy, modern people are going to love this technology! Many of us have fast-paced jobs, active families, and jam-packed schedules, so if an assistant can take some things off our plate, we'll find that to be extremely valuable.

Having an easy-to-talk-to assistant handle logistics will help people be more effective in their jobs, and eventually, people with an excellent assistant by their side will have an advantage in the hiring process. I imagine the interview of the future will include questions about how the candidate uses his or her assistant to manage work—employers will realize they're getting a bonus if they hire a skilled person *and* her skilled assistant.

Digital assistants will support busy people at work, and they will also help us pay attention to our health. Integrated with the devices we use every day, our assistants could detect low blood sugar or blood pressure fluctuations. They might even sense when we're getting stressed and suggest we take a short walk.

COMPUTER VISION

Computer vision will bring advances in a variety of fields, because there's visual data everywhere. It's not all detectable by the human eye, but with a computer that can understand images and video and process information from the world around them, we'll be able to improve everything from medical procedures to traffic control.

Historically, better technology has increased the human life span, and that trend is likely to continue. In the future, AI will be used to treat and even cure diseases. A group of dermatology researchers at Stanford University, for instance, has used new image processing capabilities—courtesy of Google's open-source machine-learning AI platform, Tensorflow—to diagnose skin conditions. They trained a model to identify cancerous skin conditions by looking at a photograph of the lesion. The model was accurate 91 percent of the time, which is about as often as the top board-certified doctors.

Computer vision will also be key to the proliferation of self-driving cars. I expect fewer and fewer people will own cars in the future—we'll just access an app, and a self-driving car will come pick us up.

FACIAL RECOGNITION

Biometric feedback may someday let us determine the

degree of customer satisfaction just by the expression on their face. If someone frowns when they look at their search results, we'll know they aren't happy. We can use that information to improve those results. It may seem like that's a long way off, but Google has had a patent on biometric feedback tech related to search results since 2012!

ROBOTICS

Currently, there are a number of domestic robots that utilize AI to perform household tasks, but they are very limited to a specific task. Take, for instance, the Roomba from iRobot, a robotic vacuum cleaner that vacuums the house for you. It learns over time where everything is at by exploring the house, and it can be set to automatically perform its task while you're gone. While there are some early robotic integrations with assistants, they are mostly just toys and are very linear in what they can do like the Roomba.

I hope I'm in the position to see robotic digital assistants come into their own in the future—the kind that can do laundry, dishes, take out the recycling, and clean the house so I will have more time to exercise, be with my family, and get other work done. Like our phones, the robotic assistants could integrate with our other assistants to streamline our lives.

BUSINESS OPPORTUNITIES

Businesses need to embrace these changes as fast as— or, ideally, faster than—the people who use them. If you're able to deliver to your customer earlier and more effectively than other businesses, you'll get first-mover advantage in the market.

The payoff will be huge. As customers move from entering searches to utilizing tech that is always on, listening and gathering information about how it can provide more value to them, search volume will soar because assistants will go out and look for information it understands the customer wants. No more waiting for the customer to make the first move! **For this reason, I expect search volume will increase twenty to thirty times over the next ten years.**

While taking care not to come across as intrusive, we'll be able to reach out to those customers via a wider range of methods, from phone and email to text and push messaging. All of these efforts will drive people further down the funnel. Ultimately, increased search volume will increase the number of purchases made, which will help businesses grow, and will stimulate the economy. How are you positioned to capitalize on this opportunity?

With personalized, predictive, and proactive technology, we'll not only generate a larger audience but also a more tailored audience. As technology continues to advance, we'll get much better at understanding the customer journey because we can utilize artificial intelligence to analyze large amounts of data; we can understand where our customers spend time online, what they're doing, and when you should reach out with what message. With enough data, we will be able to predict at a high probability the effectiveness of our campaigns—we'll know that if we invest money in campaign X, our return on investment will range from Y to Z.

In the next five to ten years, we can expect digital assistants to become more and more like high-level executive assistants. We'll have to train them a bit, but they will come to us with the world's knowledge at their fingertips and presets that make the training easy. They will interact more and more conversationally and be able to provide even more value, thanks to technological advances from people like Ray Kurzweil.

Obviously, the digital assistant won't be human. It won't have emotions. It won't have to eat or go to the restroom. It's going to be amazing to have assistants that get to know people, understand their needs, and take some tasks off their plates. It's really not a tough sell—why spend all that time grocery shopping every week when the list is always pretty much the same? Instead, you can let your assistant make the list, ask you if you want to add to it, place the order and (eventually) put the groceries away once they're delivered. Who wouldn't want that?

Other uses will be more specialized. Bank of America, for instance, has a digital assistant; customers can ask about their balance, transfer money, or get their credit scores by talking to the assistant. As more companies and brands adopt their own digital assistants, we will see them becoming very specific. One assistant might be a personal trainer coaching someone toward their fitness goals, while another one will schedule their meetings.

Over the next ten years, assistants will become increasingly integrated with our televisions, speakers, refrigerators, and other everyday devices. We're probably still five to ten years away from having an actual robot helper around the house that can do multiple tasks like mopping the floors *and* putting away the dishes, but that's coming, too. As we move toward this futuristic vision, users will have a more seamless, intuitive experience with their assistants.

I think all businesses should be following the three Ps. We should be working on being more personalized to our individual customers. We should get to know our customers, understand their needs, and then make sure that we're communicating and providing more value to them. We need to predict their needs in advance and deliver on those. Then we need to proactively do these things for the customer, rather than waiting for them to recognize a need and come to us.

CONCLUSION

FUTURE PROOF YOUR MARKETING

Throughout this book, we've discovered that every marketing strategy should be centered on the customer. Customer-centric marketing ensures that the better we understand the customer's needs and behavior, the better we can align our strategy to get the right message in front of the right people at the right time. Not only does this help you win at marketing now, but by keeping your finger on the pulse of the customer and continually monitoring their journey, you will be able to adapt as their needs and behaviors change.

We've seen that the customer's journey is about to change significantly with the arrival of new technology, particularly intelligent digital assistants. You will gain a bigger competitive advantage by leveraging the information I've shared with you: anticipate their future needs, deliver exceptional customer experiences, and strategically position yourself to take advantage of the macro trends that are driving this change. If you do these things, you will stay ahead of the competition.

The companies that will thrive in tomorrow's digital age are the ones that are strategically positioning themselves *now* to maximize the opportunities ahead of them. They are leveraging their deep understanding of their customers and their fast-paced journey to proactively predict their needs and deliver personalized experiences.

Wayne Gretzky once said, "Skate to where the puck is going, not where it has been." We all need to be managing two businesses: the current business (to maintain its success) and the one we need to become to be successful in the future.

To make it in the new marketing landscape, companies need to do the following:

- Obsess over your customer (know them better than your competition)
- Know the customer's journey
- Develop a comprehensive customer-centric marketing strategy
- Continually execute on your strategy to develop a

strong online presence and brand recognition in your industry

- Provide tremendous value for your ideal customer
- Create high-quality content that illuminates that value
- Make sure to measure meaningful metrics (what gets measured gets managed)
- Monitor the above items and predict your customers' needs so you can deliver personalized solutions proactively

Do that and you will reap these rewards:

- Measurable results
- More customers (and more "brand champions")
- More revenue
- More opportunities to achieve your purpose and have a positive impact
- Pride in your brand

If you hesitate to do these things, you're going to be like a racehorse that starts running after the other horses have already taken a couple of laps—it's hard to catch up, no matter how great a racer you are. You might be tempted to take shortcuts to run across the field and catch up, but you can hurt yourself that way. It's crucial to get out of the gate quickly and set a strong pace.

If you're not on the new digital marketing "racetrack" at

all, honestly, you risk going out of business, much like the publications that refused to transition to digital media in the mid-2000s. You want to be more like the new businesses that sprung up during that time because they learned how to navigate the changes in consumer behavior and technology. Even if you don't go out of business, you will struggle if you lag behind where consumers and technology are going. Your brand will suffer, your relevance will fall, and your revenue will decrease.

The good news is, you can decide to take action now and develop a solid strategy for your business that takes into account the coming changes. You might think your company is sufficiently well established, large enough, or popular enough that this doesn't apply to you, but from my experience, no company can afford to proceed without a well-thought-out strategy.

Customer experience (satisfaction) will be a very heavily weighted factor in this new digital age, as it should be. Now, let me ask you a simple question. If you were referring your friends to a business and they weren't having a good experience, how long would you continue to do that? Not very long, I'm guessing. Search engines have been doing everything in their power to understand and utilize customer experience so they can make the best recommendations to their customers, including utilizing over 200 different ranking factors. The digital assistants of the future will be significantly better at understanding the customer experience. The fact that they'll always be on and you won't have to do much of anything for them to understand your experience will make them even more effective. Remember, it's like having a real personal assistant with you. They'll eventually be able to understand your experience without your even saying anything—they'll just base it on your biometrics.

I personally love this. For too long, businesses that don't care about their customers and provide an inferior product or service have been taking advantage of people. In the future, this will be much harder to do and remain in business.

The path to success is simple. When you obsess over your customer, develop a successful marketing strategy, execute it effectively, commit to providing the best product/service in your industry and when you measure meaningful metrics, your business will experience incredible success and so will your clients.

To help you on your path, I've included additional resources, tools, and information in the following pages. I wish you the best in all of your future endeavors!

SUPPLEMENT

As you look to develop and implement your new customer-centric strategy, you might have the internal resources to do it all on your own, or you might be looking to find someone to partner with to fill some expertise gaps.

If you choose to partner with an expert or experts, here are a few tips:

HOW TO HIRE THE RIGHT MARKETING AGENCY

- Ask the potential agency to do an initial analysis of your website and online presence. Many agencies will do an automated audit that provides some value. This should be free, but depending on the level of detail, they may charge you for this service. At Webfor, if we believe you to be a good potential fit as a client, we will do an initial analysis at no charge. Having done this for over a decade, we expect to uncover a minimum of $5,000 in value during this process. However, we've freely given information to clients that could easily mean millions of dollars to them. Our goal is always to drench you in value.

- This initial analysis will be very helpful for you to understand how the agency works and to get an idea of their expertise. The hard part is not knowing what you don't know. For instance, whether they left something out that may be critical, and whether that's because they have a lack of expertise in a particular area or because they just don't offer the service. As we discussed, it's best to have your tactics and teams integrated, instead of siloed, for maximum effectiveness. For example, if you're running PLA (Product Listing Ads or Google Shopping Ads), you're unable to set up keyword targeting as you can in other ad types. At Webfor, our SEO specialist will often work with our paid specialist and web developer to optimize the individual pages, as well as the product feed, to make the ad campaigns more effective. We've found that SEO and paid work really well together when they aren't working against each other.

- If you're hiring an SEO agency, Google itself provides some tips at https://support.google.com/webmasters/answer/35291?hl=en.

- Start out with the right mindset. Many companies go looking for a vendor and ultimately that's what they get. They wonder why they're having such a hard time finding an agency that can help them reach their goals. Stop looking for a vendor and start looking for a partner—someone who is going to be critical to the success of your business and with whom you find mutual value and respect. This is the key to a successful long-term relationship.

- Speaking of keys to long-term relationships, you will want to discuss the following three areas and make sure it's a two-way street:
  - Expectation: The biggest threat to a long-term relationship is misaligned expectations. So many people have a blueprint in their mind of how things are going to unfold. It's important that the partner you work with sets clear expectations with you. It is equally critical that you communicate to the agency that you will be highly responsive to their requests for information and deliver what they need in a timely manner. This will be a breath of fresh air for them and help put the relationship on the right foot. It shows that you're committed to engaging in an effective working partnership. There is a direct correlation between having strong mutual engagement with your marketing agency and successfully meeting the marketing objectives of your company.
  - Communication: Communication is critical to the success of any project where more than

one person is involved. How does the agency communicate with you? What is the cadence of meetings—monthly, weekly? What if you need to reach someone right away? What if you run into an issue or aren't happy with how things are going? How will they work with you to resolve that?

- Value: At the end of the day, both parties should be receiving value out of the relationship. If one isn't committed, the marketing partnership will fail. For example, a big part of the value you're giving to the agency is the retainer or payment for their services. Paying this on time shows you respect and appreciate them. The agency should be providing tremendous value to you as well. You should discuss what value you hope to receive and how you can work together to make sure that value is being tracked and delivered.

- What questions are they asking you? The questions an agency asks can tell you a lot about their focus. Are they asking you questions that really get to the heart of understanding your business, or are they more focused on their own interests?

- The digital marketing space is complex with many different strategies and tactics. Unfortunately, many businesses have popped up that prey on businesses' lack of digital marketing background and knowledge.

- Check their online reviews. Call three of their clients.

- Check their online presence.
- If you're hiring an agency that will be writing content or posting to social for you, find out how they intend to write with a voice that reflects your company's culture.
- How will they work with or complement your internal team?
- Do they have experience with your type of product or service?
- Ask them how they will measure success.

AVOID THESE COMMON MISTAKES

- Stay away from companies that "guarantee results." While this can be enticing for businesses, it is just a marketing hook that reputable companies don't use. Google itself warns, "Beware of SEOs that claim to guarantee rankings, allege a 'special relationship' with Google, or advertise a 'priority submit to Google.'"
- Avoid unsolicited phone calls and emails. While a small percentage of them may be from reputable agencies, the majority are scams or low-quality vendors.
- Going with the low-cost provider. We've seen this mistake happen over and over. We get it, budgets are limited, but you're just falling for a sales tactic.

I'm not saying you'll need to hire marketing help from an

agency—you might have the right people in-house and the right perspective and resources to be able to implement your strategy on your own. That's great. If you do decide you need outside guidance, though, I encourage you to do your due diligence.

Whatever you do, it's time to get started. Take the action you need to *Future Proof Your Marketing*, because the future of digital is now!

APPENDIX

Webfor.com/top-tools-list

ADDITIONAL DOWNLOADABLE WHITE PAPERS AND WORKSHEETS

- The Customer-Centric Digital Strategy Worksheet: Webfor.com/strategy-worksheet
- The 5WH Social Media Worksheet: Webfor.com/social-strategy-worksheet
- Unique Value Proposition (worksheet): Webfor.com/uvp
- SEO 101 Whitepaper: Webfor.com/seo-white-paper
- Ideal Customer Profile Worksheet (Persona): Webfor.com/ideal-customer

A LIST OF SOME OF MY FAVORITE RESOURCES AND TOOLS

RESOURCES

- Moz SEO Learning Center
- Search Engine Land
- Content Marketing Institute

TOOLS

Search Engine Optimization: Organic Search

- Google Trends
- KeywordTool.io
- Answer the Public
- Google Keyword Planner: You'll need to sign up for a Google Ads account, but that's free
- SEMrush: One of my favorite all-around tools that spans SEO, content, paid, and more
- Screaming Frog
- Sitebulb
- Google Search Console
- Ahrefs
- BuzzSumo
- Moz
- SimilarWeb (competitive analysis tool)
- BrightLocal
- Majestic

Paid Ad Management

- Wordstream
- SEMrush
- Google Ads
- Bing Ads
- Facebook Ads (works for Instagram, too)
- Twitter Ads
- Reddit Ads (yes, Reddit has ads)

Analytics

- Google Analytics (free, robust website analytics tool)
- Google Tag Manager: Free tag manager tool to manage the multiple tracking code snippets installed on one's website, as well as to improve overall performance and tracking
- Google Data Studio
- Kissmetrics

User Data and Research

- CrystalKnows: Run a DISC personality profile on publicly available online information, such as a person's LinkedIn profile. This allows you to understand how your customer communicates and thinks
- Claritas: Browse the already heavily researched personas, or as they call them, segments, to see if your customers fall in the prebuilt audience types. You can

also use the ZIP Code Look-up tool to obtain information about top consumer segments in your area

- SurveyMonkey: Create a free survey to gather information from your customer base. If you have no customer base or are going into a new market, they have millions of people ready to take surveys whom you can survey, for a cost
- Facebook Audience Insights
- Uxpressia: Create personas and customer journey maps

Social Media Marketing (PR and Influencer)

- Hootsuite
- Sprout Social
- Mention.com
- Rival IQ
- Quuu
- Buffer.com

Email Marketing and Marketing Automation

- MobileMonkey (chatbot)
- Mailchimp: Email marketing tool that is free for up to 2,000 subscribers
- Drip.com
- Drift.com

Content, Conversion Rate Optimization, and User Experience

- Google Optimize: Free tool that allows you to run A/B split testing on your website
- Mobile Website Speed Testing Tool: https://testmysite.thinkwithgoogle.com/
- Mobile Website Friendliness Testing Tool: https://search.google.com/test/mobile-friendly
- Google PageSpeed (another website speed testing tool): https://developers.google.com/speed/
- Unbounce: Landing page creation tool
- Hotjar
- Crazy Egg
- Optimizely
- Vwo.com
- Usertesting.com
- UsabilityHub.com
- Uberflip.com

ABOUT THE
AUTHOR

KEVIN GETCH, Webfor's founder and director of digital strategy, started his career in marketing over sixteen years ago. He has been quoted and published in leading sites like Forbes, Huffington Post, Search Engine Journal, and Mashable. Kevin speaks at industry conferences and serves on the board of directors for SEMpdx, a nonprofit organization focusing on connecting and educating people in the digital marketing community. For his work, Kevin was a recipient of the Vancouver Business Journal's Accomplished and Under 40 award. Kevin lives in Vancouver, Washington, and enjoys practicing mixed martial arts and spending time with his wife and two kids.